A Book of Honey

EVA CRANE
A BOOK OF HONEY

Charles Scribner's Sons

New York

1980

Contents

Preface

The first four chapters of this book tell the story of honey from its raw materials to its uses and applications. Chapter 1 describes how bees find and collect the raw material and convert it into honey, and explains why they make honey – a high-energy food that can be stored almost indefinitely. It also explains why plants attract bees, and how bees benefit them. Chapter 2 describes the plant materials (mainly nectar and honeydew) from which honey is made, and explains what constitutes a good honey plant, and why. Where the common name of a plant is used without its botanical name, this can be found through the index entry for the common name; it is given in full there, or on the first page listed.

In Chapter 3 honey itself is investigated: what honey typically consists of, and its never-ending variations – according to plant source, flow conditions, beekeeping management, and the bees themselves. Flavour and aroma, sweetness, hardness or softness, and colour: all depend on the constituents of honey, and 181 substances have so far been identified in it. These substances are discussed, and related to the plant sources and to the bees' contributions to the honey.

Chapter 4 describes some of the many uses for honey in the home, and includes recipes for cooked and uncooked dishes made with honey, for mead made by fermenting honey into alcohol, and for first aid remedies and cosmetics.

Honey has a long and fascinating history, some of which is recounted in Chapter 5, from the Miocene period 10–20 million years ago when flowering plants and social bees first came into existence. Man has left records of his honey-harvesting activities since the end of the Ice Ages, 10,000 years ago. Pictorial, written, and finally printed evidence brings the story up to the present, when honey is a world commodity with an annual production of 800,000 tons.

Bees have always held an important place in the minds of men, and Chapter 6 recalls their sacred status in the Ancient World. Their religious significance lived on through the centuries, old beliefs being joined by new ones, like 'telling the bees'. References in literature give interesting sidelights on the value accorded to bees through the centuries – and to the honey and wax they produce.

Some readers may want to consider starting to keep bees so that they can harvest their own honey, and Appendix 1 provides basic information that will enable them to decide whether this is a practical proposition for them.

Appendix 2 provides a data bank of facts and figures for reference, and beekeepers, teachers and students may find that they use this section of the book more constantly than any other. Finally, there is a list of books for further reading under the separate Chapter headings. Books mentioned only briefly in the text are described there more fully. The book referred to as *Comprehensive survey* is *Honey: a comprehensive survey*, edited by Eva Crane (Heinemann in cooperation with the International Bee Research Association, 1975).

Various members of my staff at the International Bee Research Association, especially Penelope Walker, have participated in one way or another in the production of this book, and I record here my great appreciation for their help and support. Frank Vernon photographed the honey pots shown on the cover: they are described on pages 66–68.
1980

E.C.

Acknowledgements

Fig. 1 Reproduced with permission from Dorothy Hodges (1974) *The pollen loads of the honeybee*, International Bee Research Association; Figs. 2, 12, 14 Drawings by Dorothy Hodges; Figs. 3, 4, 5, 10, 11, 24 Drawings by Richard Lewington; Figs. 6, 7 Reproduced with permission from V.C. Thompson (1960) 'Nectar flow and pollen yield in south-western Arkansas, 1945-1951', *Rep. Ser. Ark. Agric. Exp. Sta.*, No. 94; Fig. 8 Reproduced with permission from E. Amaral (1957) 'Honeybee activities and honey plants in Brazil', *American Bee Journal*, 97(10) pp. 394-395; Fig. 9 adapted with permission from Dorothy Hodges (1958) 'A calendar of bee plants', *Bee World* 39(3) pp. 63-70, fig. 2; Fig. 17 Copy by Harald Pager (Johannesburg), IBRA Collection; Fig. 18 Reproduced with permission from Lya R. Dams (1978) 'Bees and honey-hunting scenes in the Mesolithic rock art of eastern Spain', *Bee World* 59(2) pp. 45-53; Fig. 19 Reproduced with permission from D.H. Gordon (1960) *The pre-historic background of Indian culture* 2nd ed. fig. 14/1, Bombay: N.M. Tripachi; Fig. 20 Reproduced from J.G. Krünitz (1774) *Das Wesentlichste der Bienen-Geschichte und Bienen-Zucht*, Berlin: Joachim Pauli; Fig. 21 Reproduced with permission from G. Kuény (1950) 'Scènes apicoles dans l'Ancienne Égypte', *J. Near Eastern Studies* 9:84-93, fig. 2; Fig. 22 Reproduced from Sebastian Münster (1544) *Cosmographia*, Basel; Fig. 23 Reproduced from F.G. Jenyns (1886) *A book about bees*, p. 51, London: Wells, Gardner, Darton & Co.; Fig. 25 Reproduced with permission from Hilda M. Ransome (1937) *The sacred bee in ancient times and folklore*, London: George Allen & Unwin Ltd., p. 150; Fig. 26 Reproduced from Virgil, *The Fourth Book of the Georgics*, trans. John Dryden (1697), copy in IBRA library.

1. Bees: the honey producers

HONEYBEES

It is easy to imagine that bees produce honey all through the summer – in fact whenever they are 'busy' flying – and that the beekeeper takes some of the honey when he wants to, but this is far from the truth. What actually happens is much more intricate, and much more interesting. The hive bee or honeybee, *Apis mellifera*, that makes most of the world's honey, has many capabilities as an individual, and a colony of these bees living in a hive as an integrated social unit has many more.

All honey has its origin in certain plant materials (mainly nectar and honeydew) which foraging bees find and collect, and which is made into honey in the hive. The bees of the hive constitute a colony, and at its height the numbers might be something like this:

reproductive
     1 queen (female)
   300 drones (male)
non-reproductive females
25,000 older workers, foragers
25,000 young workers in the hive. These rear the brood which
      might consist of:
  9,000 larvae requiring food
  6,000 eggs (from which future larvae will hatch)
20,000 older larvae sealed in cells, which need no attention
      except to be kept warm.

The older worker bees of a colony are available for foraging only if there are enough young workers to feed the brood and to keep the brood-nest temperature steady at 34°–35°C (93°–95°F). As well as the raw materials for honey, the foragers must also collect sufficient pollen to provide protein for the developing brood. So the honey-getting capacity of a colony depends on the total population of bees in it, and on the balance between different age groups.

A good beekeeper can recognize signs of balance or imbalance – for instance too little brood being reared – and his experience enables him to get his colonies in the right condition for the onset of each major 'flow' of nectar or honeydew. With a large force of foragers at that time, the colony (and the beekeeper) can obtain the maximum advantage from the flow.

INDIVIDUAL BEES

The performance of bees is truly astonishing. The fuel consumption of a flying bee is about $\frac{1}{2}$ mg honey per kilometre, or 3 million km to the litre. In providing one kilogram of surplus honey for market, the colony has had to consume something like a further 8 kg to keep itself going, and the foraging has probably covered a total flight path equal to six orbits round the earth – at a fuel consumption of about 25 g of honey for each orbit. In British units, this means 7 million miles to the gallon; a pound of honey on the breakfast table necessitates a total flight path equivalent to three orbits round the earth, each orbit using up an ounce of honey as fuel.

All behaviour of bees is instinctive, and to speak of their work, tasks, duties, and even division of labour, is to endow the bees with an intelligence and a consciousness they do not possess. It is nevertheless understandable that bees should be spoken of in this way, for the complex set of behaviour patterns referred to as the 'organization of the colony' is truly remarkable.

Most of the bees are workers, non-reproductive females. The chief factors that determine an individual worker's actions are the needs of her colony, and her own age – not her calendar age but her physiological age, which determines what she can do (Table 2 in Appendix 2). When she first emerges from her cell as an adult bee, or imago, she is not fully mature physiologically (nor is the drone, the male bee). None of the glands that will control her specialized behaviour in later life are yet developed. She moves across the combs, cleaning cells, eating honey or nectar and pollen, the latter providing the protein that enables the hypopharyngeal glands in her head to develop. These glands then produce bee milk, and the bee starts to feed larvae, and also possibly the queen, with the milk. The glands may be active from around the fifth to the tenth day after emergence. As they atrophy, the wax glands under her abdomen mature; the bee secretes wax, and takes part in comb building and repairing. As the wax glands decline (around the fifteenth day), the venom glands become active, and the bee is likely to be found near the hive entrance in a 'defence' posture, and ready to attack any approaching enemy. Then the hypopharyngeal glands, that secreted bee milk in the young worker but are now atrophied, produce a secretion rich in the enzymes diastase, invertase and glucose oxidase, that take part in the conversion of nectar into honey. Invertase production reaches a maximum in foraging bees when they are about four weeks old; it is much reduced in winter and increases again in spring.

The first three of these glandular secretions of bees are all harvested and marketed. Bee milk is what is popularly called royal jelly. Methods for harvesting it from the hive were devised in the 1950s, and it was sold as a dietary supplement or, subject to the laws of each country, for its supposed medicinal benefits. Preparations containing royal jelly are still on sale in some countries, often at a price much higher than is warranted even by the great amount of work involved in its production.

Beeswax is very much easier to harvest; the bees' combs are built of it. A high temperature is required for prolific wax secretion, and most is produced in tropical regions, especially in Africa. The whole of the comb is harvested from primitive hives in use there, and the beeswax yield is usually 8 per cent of the honey yield; in most modern beekeeping wax production is deliberately suppressed, and is likely to be $1\frac{1}{2}$–2 per cent of the honey yield. About 10,000 tons appear on the world market each year, but this amount is still insufficient to meet the demand.

Bee venom is harvested because it has pharmacological properties. A bare wire is stretched across a thin membrane fixed in front of a hive entrance. When an electric current is passed through the wire, bees coming out of the hive receive a mild electric shock which stimulates them to sting the delicate membrane. They are able to withdraw their sting and are thus

1. Bees collecting pollen from willow catkins (*Salix caprea*). The bee on the left is scraping pollen from the anthers with her mandibles, and the bee in flight is transferring honey from her tongue to the pollen (moistening it), and packing it on to combs of stiff hairs on her hind legs. The bee hanging by a foreleg is shaping her pollen loads with her middle legs.

unharmed, but they leave a drop of venom on the underside of the membrane, whence it is collected.

We do not yet fully understand what impels the bee to move to, and remain within, the appropriate part of the hive: the brood nest, the honey store above it, or where new comb is being built. It may be the bee's sensitivity to certain stimuli: temperature, pheromones secreted by the queen (the link with the queen becoming weaker as the worker gets older), light or darkness. In the first week or two the bee becomes less and less attracted by the darkness of the brood nest, until finally brightness begins to attract her. She then ventures outside the hive, and her wings become developed in short orientation flights.

After perhaps three weeks in the hive, with orientation flights in the final few days, the worker bee starts foraging. She is likely to collect pollen to begin with (fig. 1), and later to shift to nectar collection (fig. 2). She will continue with this activity until she dies, usually while out of the hive on a foraging trip. A worker bee may collect pollen and nectar on the same flight, and a shortage of pollen in the hive can stimulate her to forage for it. The stimuli that govern her nectar collection (the first step in honey production) are discussed later.

Foragers collect water as well. Normally only a few individuals do so, and we do not yet understand why some bees do and some do not. Some water collectors pass on to collecting nectar, but a

2. Bees foraging for nectar on white clover (*left*) and on lime (*right*). The bee alights on a clover flower head and probes each floret in turn; on the lime flower she hangs upside down and thrusts her tongue between the sepals where the nectar is secreted.

few may collect only water until they die. Some of the relatively few guard bees similarly remain at this behavioural stage, and never become foragers at all.

Foragers also collect propolis, a resinous secretion of plants – on poplar buds for instance. Propolis collectors are unusual in that they (alone among foragers) also work in the hive, where they use the propolis for repairing the hive and making it weathertight, and sometimes for reducing the size of its entrance hole. Like bee venom, propolis has various pharmacological properties, and preparations of it are marketed, especially in eastern European countries.

There is a popular idea that bees wear themselves out foraging in the field to produce honey. Most worker bees do indeed die outside the hive, as foragers, but this is because foraging is the last of all the age-linked activities that bees embark on. It is not foraging that wears bees out so much as brood rearing (secretion of brood food) in the early part of their life. In summer, when all young bees normally produce bee milk, they live only a few weeks. The colony population is renewed at the cost of the early death of its workers. But bees reared in the autumn have little or no brood to feed, and they live for six to seven months, through the winter and into the next spring. Summer bees that forage but have no brood to rear (because their colony is queenless, or the queen is caged for experimental purposes) are long-lived like winter bees. Further information is given in Appendix 2 on the general pattern of a worker bee's life (Table 2) and on her life span in relation to brood rearing (Table 3).

Many excellent films have been made of the life of a colony of bees. They include close-up sequences of most of the activities described here, which cannot be watched so easily in a hive, since bees are small and numerous and move very quickly.

THE BEE COLONY

The honeybee colony undergoes dramatic changes in the course of the year. In describing this, it is simplest to start at the end of the active season. In the north and south temperate zones this will be autumn, when the temperature is falling and day length decreasing. As the flowering season comes to an end, foragers bring back to the hive less and less nectar and, more important, less and less pollen, and brood rearing drops off.

If it becomes too cold for bees to fly, brood rearing ceases altogether, and the whole colony forms a cluster that occupies only a small fraction of the total space in the hive. The bees are not motionless, but move about within and around the cluster. In milder spells they eat the honey stored in nearby cells, and have no need of pollen. After the days begin to lengthen and the cold weather to abate, the bees are able to maintain a small patch of comb at the temperature at which brood can live and develop, around 34°–35°C (93°–95°F). The queen is fed on bee milk and starts to lay eggs. The tiny brood nest thus created is often little more than notional, and the onset of significant brood rearing is stimulated by the availability of fresh pollen. Another necessity is honey, but there will still be stores of honey in the hive. Honey is the primary food and energy source of adult bees, and their population will have dropped to perhaps half the count at the start of winter. What the colony must fetch from outside the hive in early spring is water, for honey and pollen are in themselves too concentrated for brood rearing. The value of nectar to bees at this time may sometimes depend more on the water it contains than on its sugar content.

In early spring the colony thus consists almost entirely of autumn-reared workers, which have already lived for up to half a year. These die, but in due course are more than replaced by new bees, as the queen's egg laying speeds up and the new brood is reared.

The number of bees in the colony increases with the rate of egg laying, but lags behind it somewhat. The number reaches a maximum in high summer after the emergence of brood from the peak period of egg laying. The population then drops off, but not as fast as the egg laying, because with less brood to feed the bees live longer. Indeed after egg laying ceases in the autumn, the population may remain fairly constant for a month or two because the death rate is then low. The population is reduced in early spring as the autumn-reared bees become old and die, and does not attain its most rapid spring growth until several weeks after the most rapid increase in egg laying.

HOW BEES FIND SOURCES OF HONEY

The bees' strategy in exploiting sources of honey is a complex and fascinating process in which the various senses of each bee operate, singly or in concert, according to her individual ability. The honeybee is one of many animals that can orient themselves by a wide variety of clues, any of which may be used according to circumstances. The honeybee also exhibits a social behaviour pattern of the highest level in animals that act instinctively.

The bee's various senses, especially of smell and sight, play the following roles when she is foraging.

Scent, of flowers for instance, can attract bees from some distance, and bees can remember a scent for several days. In the hive, scent can be communicated from any one bee to another within 'smelling distance'.

Bees have good colour vision, and certain colours attract them more than others, but usually from shorter distances than scent. A bee cannot remember a colour for long, and cannot communicate her knowledge of it to another bee. The spectrum of colours visible to bees lies more to short wavelengths than the human visible spectrum: blue is especially attractive (red not), and a range of ultraviolet colours invisible to man is visible, and attractive, to bees. Many flowers that appear plain white to us appear in colour patterns to bees, their patterning being in

3. A bee doing a wagtail dance on the comb, with 4 'followers'.

ultraviolet colours that we cannot see.

Certain shapes or forms attract bees, one positive feature being a long outline in relation to size; for instance the shape of a flower with five separated petals is more attractive than a simple circle. A bee can remember shapes, but cannot communicate information about them to another bee.

By their form and colour, bees can recognize and remember many objects that serve them as landmarks. A specific tree, bush, or the edge of a wood, for instance, might serve as a bee's landmark; but the bee recognizes only the appearance of the object, not its character, and she cannot communicate this appearance to other bees.

A bee can recognize and remember the sun's position in the sky, i.e. the angle between her own flight path from the hive and a horizontal line from the hive in the direction of the sun. If she finds good forage on this flight path, she is likely, when she returns to the hive, to carry out a 'wagtail dance' (fig. 3) on the vertical comb surface, the 'wagtail run' of the dance bearing the same angle to the upward vertical on the comb as her flight path bore to the sun's azimuth. The bee 'translates' the horizontal direction of the sun to the vertical direction of (or rather against) gravity. Other bees can sense and remember the vertical angle, and can fly out from the hive in the same direction as that taken by the first bee that found the forage. So direction of flight is communicated from bee to bee.

A bee can recognize her energy expenditure on a flight. In normal circumstances this gives a measure of the distance she has flown, although not if she flew steeply up or down hill, or with or against a strong wind. In her dance in the hive, the tempo is more vigorous if the food she flew to was close to the hive, and there is a direct relationship between the time for one wagtail run and the distance of the food. If the distance is very large, the dance is lethargic, or may not take place at all. Distance in this sense can be remembered, and communicated to other bees, so those flying in the same direction as the bee that found the food source, can fly

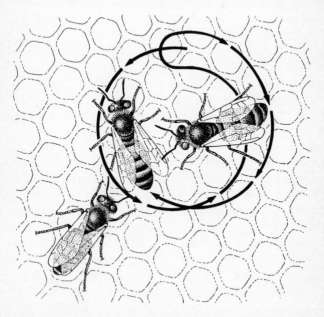

4. A bee doing a round dance on the comb, with 2 'followers'.

for the same distance and find the food.

Bees have a good time sense and a good time memory. If they find a rich food source at a certain place at one time of day only, they are likely to visit the same place at the same time next day, and every day thereafter until the food is no longer available. This is important to them, since many flowers secrete nectar only for a short period each day, either in the morning or in the afternoon. A bee finding honey at your out-door breakfast table, for instance, is likely to reappear each day so long as you do not change your breakfast time. Bees cannot communicate time as such, but all bees in the hive work to the same 'clock'.

A bee returning to the hive from flowers yielding nectar has, stored in her memory, the scent, colour and shape of the flowers, their distance and direction from the hive, and the time of day at which she found the nectar. When she dances in the hive, other bees can learn the position and scent of the flowers, although not their colour or shape. Each dance circuit takes only a few seconds; the time has the following sort of relationship with the distance from which the forager has brought the food in her honey sac:

Distance (metres)	200	500	1,000	2,000	3,500	4,500
Duration of each wagtail circuit (seconds)	2·1	2·5	3·3	3·8	5·6	6·3

If the food source is very close to the hive, less than say 50–100 metres, the forager performs a simpler movement known as a 'round dance' (fig. 4). This may be regarded as a general excitement or alerting dance, from which other bees – potential 'recruits' to work the crop – learn that good forage is available close to the hive; they also learn its scent from the dancing forager.

The efficiency of the dance communication can be quite high. In some experiments where a rather low efficiency might be expected, of 339 bees that 'followed' one marked dancer returning with food from 100 metres, 152 were kept under continuous observation. Of these 152, 56 remained in the hive and 96 flew out, of which 58 (60 per cent) found the food, most of them within a few minutes of leaving the hive.

When a bee is excited by a dance to seek out certain flowers in a certain place, she can find them; when she does so she learns their colour and shape. She is called a 'recruit' or 'newcomer'; the bee from whom she learns may well be an established forager.

We have seen that foraging is the final activity in a worker bee's life. A common pattern in the bee's initiation to foraging is that she becomes excited by the scent of a returning forager dancing on the combs, from whom she may also receive a taste of the new nectar. The recruit may go out searching for this scent, and find the same patch of flowers or another similar one. She actually has the ability to fly to the place indicated by the direction and tempo of the dance, even though she herself has not yet performed a dance. If the nectar flow is a rich one, the recruit bee is likely to become fixed on this particular flow, and she will then work it as an established forager, dancing when in the hive and thus stimulating more recruits to work the same crop. She is likely to work quite a small area of the crop as long as it is yielding nectar, and even until she dies – a single flowering tree, one row of raspberries, or a single patch of clover. During a single flight the area covered is very much smaller. This constancy is the basis of the bee's effectiveness as a pollinator (see page 21).

A less common pattern is that the new forager does *not* visit crops she learns about from established foragers. Instead she scouts around for sources of food, being attracted to them by their colour and scent. Such scout bees are of foraging age but do not belong to any special age group within it. A scout may at any time become fixed to a nectar source she finds, turning into an established forager. But some individuals behave as scouts for their whole foraging period. Bees show a continuous spectrum of behaviour, although many of them work one crop until it is finished and are then recruited to another. All types are useful to the colony, from the one that extracts as much as possible from dwindling resources, to the one that discovers new sources of food as old ones disappear.

As far as we know, a bee registers the distance of the *outward* journey to the food source, or more precisely the energy used on this flight. Before flying out from the hive she loads up with food that serves as fuel for the outward journey, and if the food she will collect is a long way off she takes a bigger load than if it is close by. But the flight direction she registers is the one on the *homeward* journey. A bee registers the colour and shape of the source of nectar as she approaches it, not when she leaves it. She learns the colour during the two seconds before and two seconds after she first dips her proboscis in the liquid food. Her learning of flower colour is reinforced many times as she takes nectar from successive flowers or florets of the same plant. The bee assesses the richness of nectar by its taste, presumably by its sweetness, not by its food value, and this assessment is made while she is imbibing the nectar.

The above is a brief and simplified summary of the subject, of which several well written more detailed accounts are available in *The dancing bees* and *The dance language and orientation of bees* by K. von Frisch (see *Further Reading* section, Chapter 1).

COLLECTING THE NECTAR

A foraging bee flies at about 21–24 km/hour (13–15 mph), at a height of between one and eight metres above the ground. If it is windy she may fly even lower, where she will get more shelter, and she is unlikely to set out at all in a wind much above 24 km/hour. She will fly higher if necessary to surmount small obstacles (trees, a hill, or buildings), but larger obstacles tend to deter her: in a mountain valley, for instance, she will tend to fly along the valley rather than over the hills that bound it. The air-space above 15 metres or so (depending on the weather) is used only by queens and drones; a worker flying there would run the risk of being harassed by drones, although this would be an unproductive exercise on their part, since mating would be impossible.

The forager will have taken with her enough nectar from the hive to enable her to reach the crop she is working, and she can locate it without difficulty, so she flies direct to the crop and visits one flower after another until her honey sac is full.* The flower of the tulip poplar, *Liriodendron tulipifera*, holds so much nectar

---

* The honey sac of the worker bee (also known as the honey bag, honey stomach or crop) is a widened part of her alimentary canal, beyond the oesophagus. Beyond the honey sac is a valve which serves to prevent nectar or honey passing through to the digestive system.

that the bee can fill her honey sac from a single visit, but this is unusual. Usually a bee visits between fifty and a thousand flowers on a trip, but it can be several thousand. These visits may take quite a long time, as the following detailed records show. During a good flow from sweet clover, *Melilotus*, when the hive was gaining 5 lb (over 2 kg) a day, an average foraging trip was found to last 34 minutes, and the next year, when the flow was less good, the average was 49 minutes. Even in the good year some foragers were away for three hours, and in the poor season it could be much longer. Other detailed observations on individual marked bees show that a quick foraging expedition might take half an hour, and longer ones up to four hours.

Clearly a bee cannot make a great many foraging trips in one day; on sweet clover the average number was 13·5 during the good flow and 7 during the poor one, and no bee made more than 24 and 17 respectively. When there is no rich flow, each forager probably makes less than 10 trips a day, and may make only 3 or 4.

The gain to the colony from each foraging trip is, of course, minute. A foraging bee weighs 80–85 mg; she can carry a load up to 70 mg in her honey sac, but even during a flow she is more likely to carry only 40 mg, and in windy weather even less. Often more than half the load is surplus water that will evaporate off in the hive. It is no wonder that bees have to be selective in choosing their sources of nectar.

How far does a bee go on a foraging trip? In the broadest terms, no further than she has to. Colonies of bees moved to new pasture start foraging close to the hive, flying further out as they become acquainted with their surroundings and as the nearby food gets used up. If forage is available within 200 or 500 metres of their hive, most bees will probably work it. In recent large-scale experiments, bees foraging on flowers were tagged with tiny, numbered discs that were later pulled off the bees as they entered their hives by a large magnet fitted at the entrance. Although bees foraging on one plant species used the area of it nearest to their hive, it was found that some bees flew several kilometres to forage on plant species that were not available nearer their hive. Like human beings, bees seem to appreciate variety in their diet. The area worked by any one colony may be restricted by competition from foragers of other colonies, and the whole foraging pattern changes constantly as existing sources dwindle and new sources become available.

At a flight speed of 24 km/hour, the flights to and from the hive take only 5 minutes for each kilometre, so if a foraging trip lasts half an hour or more, most of that time is spent actually foraging.

Assuming a foraging range of 500 m to 2 km, the honey produced in a hive comes from an area varying from 80 hectares (200 acres) to 1200 hectares (5 square miles), but the area can be even larger.

When a forager returns to the hive, she passes her nectar load to (younger) house bees, and we shall see later how they convert the nectar into honey. The forager may rest in the hive, although for a shorter time than she spent on her trip; the bees observed working the good flow from sweet clover spent on average $11\frac{1}{2}$ minutes in the hive after a 34-minute trip.

Many observations on the foraging activities of marked bees have shown a lull in flights around or just after midday, with a corresponding halt in the gain in weight of the colony. This has led to jocular references to the bees' 'lunch-time break'. Such a lull may be related to a gap in nectar secretion around high noon, a feature of plants in the tropics where honeybees evolved. In the tropics nectar secretion is a feature of the less hot early morning and evening periods; there is also the fact that when the sun is overhead the bees' system of direction-linked dances on the comb breaks down. We do not yet know the real answer.

The behaviour of the bee at each flower varies according to the type of flower she is visiting. Fig. 2 shows typical postures. The bee alights on the flower itself, if this is large enough and firm enough, but if not, she uses some firmer part of the plant within reach. When the bee alights, she brings her proboscis forward from its resting position beneath her 'chin', and inserts it into the part of the flower where nectar accumulates, such as a corolla. If nectar is present, the bee sucks up all she can before she tries out the next flower; if not, she quickly learns this and withdraws her proboscis, inserting it into another flower or floret. For some hanging flowers, the bee has to hover in the air to reach the nectar and suck it up.

Many flowers are larger than the bee visiting them, and some can provide a sheltered microclimate several degrees warmer than the air outside. The importance to a flower of a bee's visit that will lead to pollination is signified by characteristics of the flower which help the bee to find the nectar and pollen quickly. Most flowers have a radial symmetry, petals and sepals 'leading' to the centre where nectar and pollen are; some flowers have coloured or ultraviolet patterns of nectar guides that reinforce this centripetal pattern. Other flowers have scent guides, the scent becoming stronger nearer the site of the nectar. A flower such as an iris, whose nectar is found not at the visual centre but in 3 radial tubes, has such guides leading down the tubes; the visual centre is devoid of patterning that would interest a bee.

CONVERTING THE NECTAR INTO HONEY

Honey is made in the hive, above and around the brood nest where the temperature must be regulated quite closely at 34°–35°C (93°–95°F); the temperature of the honey area is normally within a few degrees below 35°. When a foraging bee arrives at the hive carrying, in her honey sac, the nectar or honeydew she has collected during her flight, it will already have been diluted with saliva containing secretions from several glands, especially the hypopharyngeal glands which contribute the enzymes used in elaborating honey: invertase, diastase, and glucose oxidase (see pages 18–19).

On entering the hive, the bee retains her nectar load until she encounters a house bee willing to take the food from her; the entire load is sometimes given to one bee, but it is usually distributed among three or more. As the bees approach each other, the forager opens her mandibles widely, and a drop of nectar appears on the upper surface of the base of her proboscis. The receiving bee then stretches out her proboscis to full length and quickly takes the nectar. During the transfer the antennae of each bee are in continual motion, stroking the antennae of the other bee. The receiving bee may also stroke the forager's head with her forefeet.

Before we follow the course of the nectar load, which from now on is handled by the house bees, it is worth examining the passing-over process in one other respect. If little nectar is coming into the hive, the forager will soon encounter a house bee which takes all or part of her load, and she can fly out again and collect another load. But during a heavy nectar flow she is likely to take longer to dispose of it – most house bees may already have full or partly full honey sacs and refuse to take any more.

In experiments with an overheated hive, when the bees' only method of cooling it was by evaporating water, house bees were observed to reject honey-sac loads of sugar syrup brought in by foragers, but to accept readily any loads of water. This situation was abnormal; the exercise of choice normally leads to the preferential unloading of foragers carrying richer (higher sugar concentration) nectars. All this interplay between bees in the hive serves as a communication system which enables the colony to get maximum benefit from the constantly changing food supplies around it.

If there is a heavy nectar flow, the receiving bee may deposit her load in a cell immediately, and it is manipulated later. In this case she holds a drop of nectar in position as a disgorging forager does, and then adds it directly to the liquid already present in the cell or, if this is empty, suspends it from the upper surface of the cell wall – hanging it up to dry, so to speak. But usually the receiving bee first manipulates the nectar in her mouthparts. In an uncrowded part of the hive she rests, with her head uppermost, and repeatedly unfolds and refolds her proboscis, exposing to the air an attenuated drop of nectar in the angle between the two parts of the proboscis. After 5–10 seconds, she sucks the drop back into her mouth. She repeats the whole process, with brief pauses, for perhaps 20 minutes, at the end of which she deposits her load in a cell. The water content of the nectar may be decreased from 55 per cent to 40 per cent by this procedure, within an hour of its arrival in the hive, and it will have received its full complement of bee enzymes.

The bees evaporate the rest of the surplus water from the liquid as it lies in the cells. In experiments when sugar solutions of various concentrations were placed in the cells of a comb, and the comb put into a hive *but screened from the bees*, the bees were able to evaporate water until the sugar concentration was over 80 per cent, as in honey. The speed of the process depended on the degree to which the cells were filled: when they were three-quarters full it took more than twice as long as when they were only one-quarter full. In the latter case, 60 per cent sugar solution became fully ripened within 48 hours, and 20 per cent sugar solution in 72 hours. Bees usually fill the cells at least half full; screened combs that had been completely filled with nectar took three or four days to become honey. In other experiments, combs of nectar in normally ventilated hives took from one to five days to ripen; additional ventilation at the top of the hive could reduce the time from five to three days, whereas reduced ventilation increased it to more than 21 days.

During a nectar flow, bees expedite evaporation from the cells by fanning, directing a current of air between the combs, and on still summer evenings one can hear this fanning in progress. One experimenter sealed all joints and cracks in a large hive full of bees, and fitted anemometers to two small openings which formed the only entrances. More air was drawn through the hive during the day than at night; the bees directed the flow by fanning, and the direction changed at irregular intervals without apparent cause. On a hot July day (mean temperature 27°C [81°F]) between 200 and 400 litres of air per minute entered the hive. In an ordinary hive a dozen strongly fanning bees, positioned across an entrance 25 cm wide, produced an air flow through the hive amounting to 50–60 litres per minute.

For a concentrated nectar like acacia, *Robinia pseudoacacia,* containing over 60 per cent sugar, relatively little water needs to be evaporated, but to produce a kilogram of clover honey, more than 2 kg of clover nectar containing 40 per cent sugar must be collected, or over 4 kg of a nectar containing only 20 per cent sugar. Nectar containing as little as 13 per cent sugar is hardly worth collecting, and indeed bees do not normally collect it, except in early spring when they need the water in it to dilute stored honey for brood rearing.

Jam makers will be familiar with the amount of energy (heat) required to evaporate sufficient water to achieve a high enough sugar concentration to ensure that the jam will keep. The evaporation of water similarly involves the bees in much work; they get the energy for this from the nectar or honey already in the hive.

When the honey has been evaporated to the lowest possible

water content, say 17–20 per cent according to atmospheric humidity and temperature, the bees fill each cell completely and 'cap' it, i.e. seal it with an airtight beeswax cover, which prevents absorption of water by the hygroscopic honey, and thus the risk of fermentation. Some races of bees 'cap wet', and others 'cap dry', leaving a slight air space between the honey and the capping, which then looks lighter in colour and is preferred by purchasers of sections, or other comb honey. The bees' manipulation of the liquid in the hive, between the initial stage when it is nectar or honeydew and the final stage when it is honey, introduces an enzyme which brings about chemical changes leading to a higher sugar content than could be achieved without the enzyme action. This is, so to speak, the 'secret' of honey. The enzyme is invertase which, with diastase and glucose oxidase, is produced by the bees' hypopharyngeal glands. Invertase 'inverts' the sucrose in the food collected into glucose and fructose. At the same time certain higher sugars are synthesized which (unlike glucose and fructose) are present in honey but not in the plant material.

The consequence of this inversion of sugars is as follows. At the temperature of the honey combs in the hive (30°C, 86°F) the solubility of glucose in a solution of fructose increases abruptly if the fructose concentration is raised above 1·5 grams per gram of water. The gram of water can then hold in solution, as well as the fructose, 1·25 grams of glucose, which is 50 per cent more than a dilute fructose solution can carry. This high glucose solubility does not operate at higher temperatures, nor at lower ones. Moreover the sugar sucrose does not have this property of high solubility. By inverting sucrose into glucose and fructose, at hive temperatures, the bees are able to produce a more concentrated solution of sugars than could otherwise be obtained – a supersaturated solution containing only around 18 per cent water. This has two clear advantages for the bees: their stored food supply is resistant to spoilage by fermentation, even during year-long storage, and it represents a high-energy pack, occupying minimal space. The long-term safe storage of food, dependent on enzyme secretion, could well be a factor in the evolution of permanent insect societies, but not much is yet known about enzyme production in primitively social insects.

Diastase, another enzyme secreted by the bee's hypopharyngeal glands, breaks down starch. Its function in bee physiology is not yet clearly understood, but it may be involved in the digestion of pollen. Diastase does not play any significant part in honey production, as invertase does, but in the next chapter we shall see that a certain significance is attached to its presence in honey.

The value of the third enzyme, glucose oxidase, has only recently been discovered. In dilute solutions the enzyme reacts with glucose, forming gluconolactone (gluconic acid, the major acid in honey) and hydrogen peroxide. The hydrogen peroxide thus produced in partly formed honey in the hive is able to protect it against bacterial decomposition until its sugar content is high enough to do this. A similar glucose oxidase system that produces hydrogen peroxide seems to be present in all bees that store honey in combs: the four species of honeybee, *Apis*, and colony-forming bumble bees and stingless bees. It is absent in social ants that maintain stores of honey in 'replete' individual ants. Hydrogen peroxide is an unstable compound, and glucose oxidase activity in some honeys is destroyed by visible light; the honey storage area of the hive is, however, almost completely dark.

THE BEES' SERVICE TO PLANTS: POLLINATION

Bees do not make honey in order that we may enjoy it, though this is what happens. Similarly, plants do not produce nectar in order that bees shall make and store honey, though this is what happens.

The many species of bees in the world are the most important group of agents that bring about the pollination of flowers. In agriculture, the honeybee is especially important for commercial crop pollination, because each colony provides a large number of potential pollinators (20,000–40,000), and because hives containing the colonies can be moved around from one crop to another. The pollination process is linked with nectar and pollen collection, and hence with honey production, in the following way.

Pollen grains are produced by the flower's anthers, each of which is at the outer end of a stamen, the flower's male sexual organ (fig. 5). When the pollen grains have matured inside the anther, the anther wall opens and the ripe pollen is discharged;

20

Self - pollination

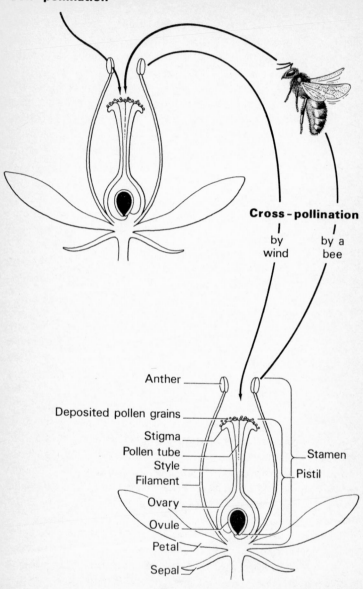

Cross - pollination

by wind

by a bee

Anther

Deposited pollen grains

Stigma

Pollen tube

Style

Filament

Stamen

Pistil

Ovary

Ovule

Petal

Sepal

5. Pollination mechanisms.

this is dehiscence. The flower's female sexual organ is the pistil, with an ovary at the base, and a style arising from it which terminates in a stigma. A ripe (receptive) stigma has a sticky surface to which pollen grains will adhere if they touch it, and the male nuclei travel through an extruded pollen tube to the ovary, where they fertilize the ovules.

The pollinator's function is to transfer the pollen from the anther to the stigma. Some plants, such as grasses, and trees bearing catkins, produce pollen that is light and dry and travels on the wind – perhaps leaving a trail of hay-fever attacks in its wake. These plants are *wind-pollinated*. Flowers of some other plants incorporate a mechanism whereby the pollen is automatically deposited on the stigma of the same flower that produced it; these are *self-pollinated*. All other plants (except the rare group in which pollen is transferred by water) need the co-operation of an animal agent. In the tropics some plants are *bird-pollinated*, but in the main, and throughout the world, they are *insect-pollinated* and, of the insects, bees are the most effective pollinators. The main reason for this is their constancy, fidelity, or faithfulness – it has various anthropomorphic names – in foraging. A foraging bee, whether a honeybee or one of the 20,000 species of wild bees in the world, normally moves from one flower to another like it, not to a different kind of flower as butterflies and many other insects do. A bee which collects nectar or pollen from a flower is likely to brush against the anther; some pollen grains adhere to her hairy body, and some of these will be captured by the sticky surface of the next stigma she touches. If this stigma belongs to a flower on a different plant of the same species, the bee has brought about *cross-pollination*. If it is on the same plant or the same clone, or genetically identical material (e.g. in grafted apple trees), then what has happened is *self-pollination*. Cross- or self-fertilization, in which the male and female gametes unite, can then follow, but pollination is its necessary precursor.

These intimate relationships in the microcosm of a flower – depending on the shape of the flower and the movement of a bee within it, on the bee's need to visit many flowers to fill her honey sac, and on her recognition of colour and her memory for scent – provide the means by which many of the world's fruit and seed crops can be harvested and increased. Cross-pollination is essential for many of these crops, and in a number of others it may give yields that are higher, of better quality, or earlier (or all three) than those produced from self-pollination. Commercial fruit crops that require insect pollination include apple, avocado, lychee, melon, passion fruit, pear, plum, sweet cherry, and water melon; two that do not are pawpaw and sweet pepper. Of nut crops, almonds must be pollinated by insects, but not peanuts. Insects are essential for producing seed crops of alfalfa (lucerne), the world's most important forage plant, and of many other legumes, for instance clovers, bird's-foot trefoil, sainfoin and sweet clover. Oil crops such as sunflower are insect-pollinated, as are coffee and seed crops of vegetables including asparagus, onion and radish. On the other hand seeds of tobacco, flax and sesame and similarly those of vegetables such as butter bean, French bean, garden pea, lettuce and lentil are produced without help from insects.

In small-scale agriculture, pollination tends to be a direct outcome of beekeeping for honey production. If, after reading Appendix 1, you start to keep bees, and no-one within 500 metres is already doing so, you may well get higher crops of such garden fruit as apple, pear, raspberry and blackcurrant, and so may your neighbours.

In large-scale agriculture the situation is different. First, monocultures of a crop that needs pollinating may cover very large areas, and hives of bees must be taken into these areas for the flowering period of the crop. They cannot, however, be left there permanently, because they would have no forage for the rest of the year. Secondly, commercial honey-producing colonies are managed so that they have a large nectar-foraging force when the flow is on. Colonies are prepared for pollination with a different aim: they should have a large amount of brood, and thus a need for much pollen, and insufficient pollen stores in the hive. This will produce a large number of pollen foragers, which are usually more effective pollinators of most plants than nectar foragers.

The tendency of most foraging bees to continue working on the same crop, instead of changing to another one, imposes an important rule on beekeepers moving bees to a crop to pollinate it: wait until the crop is in flower before moving the bees, and release them from their hives at a time of day when pollen is available from the crop. Otherwise the bees are likely to find other sources of nectar and pollen in the locality, and become fixed on them, ignoring the crop to be pollinated even when it is in full flower.

Pollen grains in honey are discussed in Chapter 3, but the significance of pollen to the colony and to the individual bee, and the behaviour pattern of pollen foraging – both subjects of great interest and importance – are beyond the scope of this book. Pollen can be harvested from bees by fixing a double grid across the hive entrance, so that incoming bees must squeeze through it, the pollen loads (pellets) attached to their hind legs being knocked off to fall into a tray below. Pollen is highly nutritious, containing proteins and vitamins, but unfortunately it is offered for sale to a public that is already well fed, at prices that are often unwarrantably high.

Honey and pollen are two hive products that result directly from the bees' foraging activities. A third is propolis, sometimes called bee glue, which bees collect for example from sticky chestnut buds, and use for making their hive or nest cavity weathertight, and for reducing its entrance. The bees contribute other materials to the nectar, pollen and propolis they collect, and process the product. Thus, honey is different from nectar and honeydew; pollen stored in the hive – known as bee bread – differs from pollen on the anthers of flowers, for instance in its much lower germinating ability; propolis is often mixed with wax before the bees use it for building and repair work.

Three other hive products, harvested commercially, are not processed plant materials, but secretions of the bees themselves. These are beeswax, produced in abdominal glands and used for building comb; royal jelly or bee milk, produced in the head glands and used for feeding larvae; and bee venom, produced in abdominal glands and used for injecting through the skin of an enemy.

Honey is the least expensive of these six materials for the beekeeper to produce, weight for weight. Next comes beeswax, then pollen, and then propolis. Royal jelly and bee venom – the most expensive of all – are harvested in minute quantities, and their production involves much hard and exacting work.

2. Plants: the honey resources

We shall now look at the general seasonal cycle of honey production and consumption by a colony of bees in a hive, as monitored by weekly records of the changes in weight of the hive with its contents. These changes represent roughly the surplus of what is brought into the hive over and above what is used up by the bees. The number of bees in the colony is also relevant, but the honey stores are likely to weigh at least ten times as much as the bees. Pollen stores also affect the weight, but much less so than does the honey, and stores of honey and of pollen tend to increase and decrease together.

In the north temperate zone no appreciable food collection is usually possible from October to April, and each week there is a loss in weight because more and more of the winter food stores are used up. The situation changes dramatically in spring, when temperatures rise and plants start to flower, and fig. 6 shows typical average weekly changes in weight through the summer. The first (and biggest) *honey flow** occurs in early May, and within a week 14 kg of surplus honey are stored. For the hives in fig. 6 the flow came from holly flowers, *Ilex opaca*. In England hawthorn and sycamore flowers might give a similar, though smaller, early flow. In other places it might be dandelion, *Taraxacum officinale*, or rosemary, acacia or rape, *Brassica napus*.

In fig. 6 the spring flow lasted a month, and other plants undoubtedly contributed to it. Then there was a lull for three

---

* More precisely, this is a *nectar* flow; a honeydew flow would give a similar although often a rather longer period of weight increase. The timing of the honeydew flow involves the population dynamics of the plant-sucking insect that produces the honeydew, and is not ruled by the flowering period of the plant.

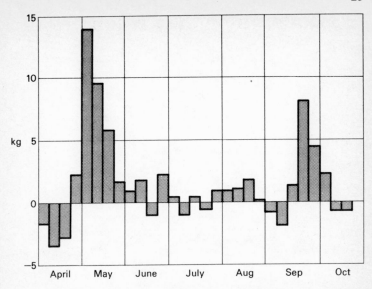

6. Average weekly gain or loss in weight of five hives at Hope, Arkansas, USA, for the four years 1948 - 1951. All entries for November to March would be losses.

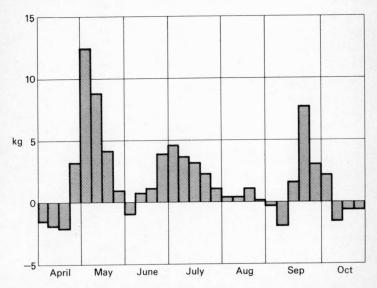

7. Average weekly gain or loss in weight of five hives at Emmet, 10 km from Hope (fig. 6), for the same period. The additional summer flow alters the annual balance from deficit to surplus.

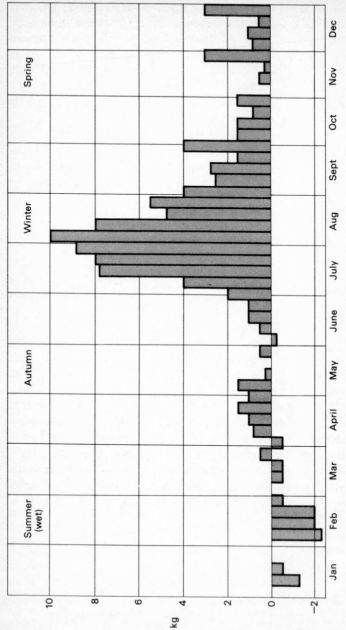

8. Average weekly gain or loss in weight of three hives at Piracicaba, Brazil, in the southern subtropics, throughout the year.

months, when the bees gained so little surplus honey that they had to break into their stores from time to time; five of the weeks show a net loss in weight. In mid-September there was a month-long late summer flow, mainly from Spanish needle, *Bidens* (Compositae), and this marked the end of the honey-producing season. The total net gain from April to September was only 11 kg, and this amount of honey would be unlikely to last the colony through the winter.

Fig. 7 shows similar hive records from a place only 10 km away, where spring and late summer flows were similar, but where there was also a long mid-summer flow from sweet clover. The net gain at the end of the season was not 11 kg, but 75 kg – enough for the beekeeper to take a harvest, say 50 kg, and leave 25 kg for overwintering.

Every place where bees are kept has its own seasonal pattern: a few honey flows that may give a surplus for the beekeeper, and a trickle of food from minor sources that helps to keep the colony going between the main flows. The 'June gap' (which lasted much longer than June in fig. 6) is a feature of most places in the north temperate zones. In general, it separates (*a*) flowering on last season's wood, or as a result of other developments in the previous season, from (*b*) flowering on the current season's wood, or as a result of other developments in the current season.

In the tropics, bees may be able to forage almost all the year, but there may be a severe dearth period – of drought, monsoon rains, or extreme heat. There will also be more copious specific flows at certain seasons. Fig. 8 shows weekly weight changes at Piracicaba in Brazil. Winter (July-September) is the honey-getting season there, and a wide variety of plants gives a continuous flow for several months. The wet summer is the dearth season, but it is short, and the colony is in deficit (consuming more than it collects) for barely three months of the year.

The total amount of food a colony brings into the hive is very difficult to assess, and no doubt varies widely. In many areas it is probably equivalent to something between 150 and 300 kg of honey, but the beekeeper can take only the honey that is surplus to the colony's own requirements – or the colony will starve. In very good bee country (e.g. Australia) the beekeeper may get one-third of the total; in parts of the world where flows are less prolific (e.g. England) he is unlikely to get more than one-tenth. This helps to explain why English honey costs more than Australian, wherever it is sold.

In general, people seem to spend more time studying honey plants and bees in areas where it is difficult to get honey, than in good honey-producing areas. Plants used by bees have been documented in exceptional detail in some countries of western Europe where honey yields are not high. Fig. 9 show the seasonal sequence of these plants in southern England; plants that can give a main flow, where enough of them are present in one locality, are marked. An area with abundant fruit blossom and dandelion, sycamore and hawthorn, raspberry and blackberry (or rape), clover, lime, and then ling heather, should yield formidable honey crops – if the weather allowed. Most commercial beekeeping in England is in areas with at least three of these flows; people who keep bees as a hobby must be content to get what they can where they live, or they may be able to increase their harvest by migrating their bees to rape say, and ling heather, *Calluna vulgaris*.

LIST OF SPECIES INCLUDED IN THE CALENDAR

1.	Laurustinus	*Viburnum tinus*
2.	Winter heath	*Erica* spp.
3.	Snowdrop	*Galanthus nivalis*
4.	Crocus	*Crocus* spp.
5.	Gorse	*Ulex europaeus*
6.	Willow	*Salix* spp.
7.	Coltsfoot	*Tussilago farfara*
8.	Blackthorn	*Prunus spinosa*
9.	Prunus	*Prunus cerasifera*
10.	Almond	*Prunus amygdalus*
11.	Celandine	*Ranunculus ficaria*
12.	Red deadnettle	*Lamium purpureum*
13.	Plum	*Prunus domestica*
14.	Cherry, sour	*Prunus cerasus*
15.	Pear	*Pyrus communis*
16.	Wallflower	*Cheiranthus cheiri*
17.	Dandelion	*Taraxacum officinale*
18.	Brassica	*Brassica* spp.
19.	Apple	*Pyrus malus*
20.	Sycamore	*Acer pseudoplatanus*
21.	Bluebell	*Endymion nonscriptus*
22.	Horse chestnut	*Aesculus hippocastanum, A. carnea*
23.	Hawthorn	*Crataegus monogyna*

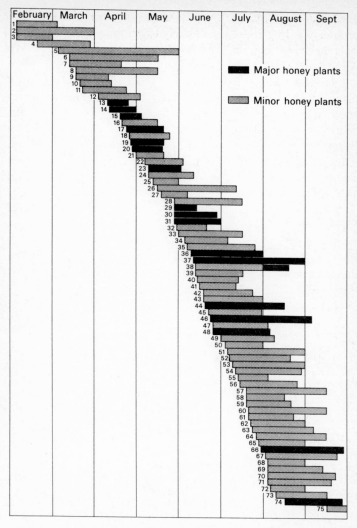

9. Approximate flowering periods of 75 plants yielding nectar and pollen. Ashtead, Surrey, England, 1940 - 1957.

24.	Cotoneaster	*Cotoneaster horizontalis* and spp.
25.	Holly	*Ilex aquifolium*
26.	White bryony	*Bryonia dioica*
27.	Broom	*Sarothamnus scoparius*
28.	Charlock	*Sinapis arvensis*
29.	Sainfoin	*Onobrychis viciifolia*
30.	Broad bean	*Vicia faba*
31.	Raspberry	*Rubus idaeus*
32.	Acacia	*Robinia pseudoacacia*
33.	Thyme	*Thymus vulgaris*
34.	Yellow melilot	*Melilotus officinalis*
35.	Cranesbill	*Geranium sanguineum, G. pratense*
36.	White clover	*Trifolium repens*
37.	Blackberry	*Rubus fruticosus*
38.	Red clover	*Trifolium pratense*
39.	Bird's-foot trefoil	*Lotus corniculatus*
40.	Bindweed	*Convolvulus arvensis, Calystegia sepium*
41.	Viper's bugloss	*Echium vulgare*
42.	Campanula	*Campanula* spp.
43.	Veronica	*Veronica spicata* and spp.
44.	Rosebay willowherb	*Chamaenerion angustifolium*
45.	Cornflower	*Centaurea cyanus*
46.	Bell heather	*Erica cinerea*
47.	Privet	*Ligustrum vulgare*
48.	Lime	*Tilia vulgaris, T. cordata*
49.	Knapweed	*Centaurea nigra*
50.	Hogweed	*Heracleum sphondylium*
51.	Borage	*Borago officinalis*
52.	White melilot	*Melilotus alba*
53.	Knotgrass	*Polygonum* spp.
54.	Field scabious	*Knautia arvensis*
55.	Sweet chestnut	*Castanea sativa*
56.	Mullein	*Verbascum thapsus*
57.	Thistle	*Cirsium arvense* and spp.
58.	Mallow	*Malva sylvestris*
59.	Marjoram	*Origanum vulgare*
60.	White charlock	*Raphanus raphanistrum*
61.	Traveller's joy	*Clematis vitalba*
62.	Sage	*Salvia officinalis*
63.	Mint	*Mentha* spp.
64.	Balsam	*Impatiens glandulifera*
65.	Chicory	*Chicorium intybus*
66.	Ling	*Calluna vulgaris*
67.	Michaelmas daisy	*Aster* spp.
68.	Purple loosestrife	*Lythrum salicaria*
69.	Toadflax	*Linaria vulgaris*
70.	Sea lavender	*Limonium vulgare*
71.	Dwarf gorse	*Ulex minor*
72.	Virginia creeper	*Parthenocissus tricuspidata*
73.	Fuchsia	*Fuchsia magellanica*
74.	Mustard	*Sinapis alba*
75.	Ivy	*Hedera helix*

NECTAR

The raw materials of honey are nectar and other natural plant exudations, which the bees collect, process and store in their combs. All these raw materials are derived from phloem sap, the fluid which moves through the tissues of a plant and transports nutrients to them.

Most of the world's honey comes from nectar, and most of this nectar is secreted by glands (nectaries) in flowers – on sepals or petals, stamens or carpels, or on other parts. Fig. 10 and fig. 11 show the floral nectaries of rosebay willowherb, *Chamaenerion angustifolium*, and of white clover, *Trifolium repens*. Some plants have nectaries elsewhere, on leaves (cherry laurel) or fronds (bracken).

The simplest nectaries are hardly distinguishable with the naked eye from surrounding plant tissues. More complex nectaries are often clearly visible, and may have quite striking shapes and

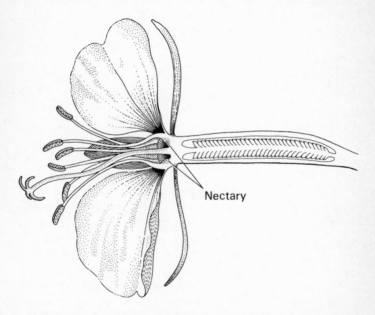

Nectary

10. Section through a flower of rosebay willowherb (*Chamaenerion angustifolium*), with one sepal, two petals and adjacent stamens removed to show the nectary at the base of the flower, between the stamens and anther.

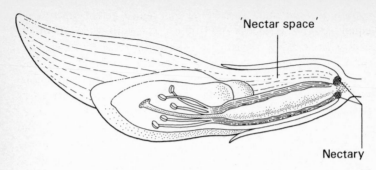

'Nectar space'

Nectary

11. Section through a floret of white clover (*Trifolium repens*), showing nectary at the base of the deep flower, between the petal and the staminal column. Secreted nectar rises up the narrow 'nectar space' if not collected, and can then be taken by an insect whose tongue is too short to reach the nectary.

colours. The function that all nectaries have in common is active secretion of nectar, the main components of which are sugars and water; nectaries have sometimes been called 'sugar valves' in that they secrete sugars and thus regulate the sugar content of the internal plant fluid. The existence of nectaries in bracken exemplifies the fact that nectaries are not confined to flowering plants. Only floral nectaries, however, have developed the secondary function of attracting pollinating insects to the flowers.

Nectar is a solution in water of various sugars, which constitute from as little as 3 per cent to as much as 87 per cent of the total weight, and 90–95 per cent of the total solid matter. It also contains very small amounts of nitrogen compounds, minerals, organic acids, vitamins, pigments, and aromatic substances. The ash content is well under 0·5 per cent. Most nectars are acid or neutral (pH 2·7–6·4), but some are alkaline (pH up to 9·1). The vitamin content of nectar is low, but it is of scientific interest that the following vitamins have been found in nectar: thiamine, riboflavin, pyridoxine, nicotinic acid, pantothenic acid, folic acid, biotin, meso-inositol and ascorbic acid (vitamin C), the only vitamin found in appreciable quantities in any nectar or honey. Primitive nectaries contain some nitrogen, especially in amino acids and amides, but the more complex nectaries contain less.

Nectars can be divided into three groups according to the sugars they contain. In one group the main sugar is sucrose (cane sugar), as it is in the phloem sap of the plant. Nectars of the second group contain sucrose, glucose and fructose, in roughly equal amounts. (Glucose and fructose, the simplest sugars of all, can be produced by inverting sucrose, for instance by the enzyme invertase.) Nectars of the third group contain glucose and fructose but hardly any sucrose; they tend to contain more fructose than glucose, and this has important consequences in determining the characteristics of the honey.

Some rhododendron nectars belong to group 1, including the Alpine rose, *Rhododendron ferrugineum*, and some Leguminosae to group 2, e.g. white sweet clover, *Melilotus alba*. Most Cruciferae and many Labiatae are in group 3, as are Spanish chestnut, *Castanea sativa*, acacia and red clover, *Trifolium pratense*, with much more fructose than glucose; and dandelion and rape have less fructose than glucose.

The sugars are the major constituents of a plant's nectar, and their total amount determines the quantity of honey that bees can produce from the nectar. In the course of their evolution bees have developed a good ability to assess the 'cost-effectiveness' of working alternative nectar sources. The attractiveness of different nectars to bees depends on the total sugar concentration, and to a certain extent on the proportions of different sugars.

Botanists measure the nectar productivity of a plant by its sugar value, the weight of sugar (in mg) secreted by one flower in 24 hours; the sugar value is fairly constant for any one plant species. Of the species that have been assessed, the following have very high values (all above 3 mg per flower in 24 hours): two limes, *Tilia platyphyllos* and *Tilia cordata*; a sage, *Salvia leucantha*; rosebay willowherb or fireweed, *Chamaenerion angustifolium*; gooseberry, *Ribes uva-crispa*; and borage, *Borago officinalis*. But sugar values have so far been measured only in Europe, and are not yet available for many of the world's very prolific honey sources, such as eucalyptus, citrus, or tulip poplar.

The total amount of honey obtainable from a plant depends on three factors: the sugar value just discussed; the number of flowers in a given area (which governs the number within reach of a colony of bees); and the number of days the flowers are secreting nectar. These factors can be combined to give a theoretical 'honey potential': the number of kilograms per hectare (or pounds per acre) of honey that could be obtained in one

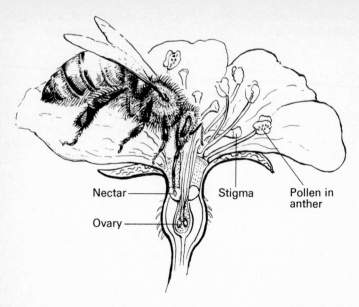

12. Section through a pear flower showing the nectary, which is easily reached by a bee standing on the flower petals.

season from land covered by the plant in question. Satisfactory plant-growth conditions for nectar production are assumed, and an adequate force of foraging bees to collect all the nectar secreted, as well as suitable weather. For some plants the honey potential works out at several hundred kg per hectare, but a hundred or so is a more common figure, even among good honey plants. As with the sugar value, estimates have been made only for plants that grow in Europe. The following are a few of the plants for which a honey potential of more than 100 kg/ha has been calculated, although in practice not all of them would cover an area as large as an acre or a hectare: borage, dandelion, acacia, rosebay willowherb and small-leaved lime.

The willingness with which bees collect nectar from any one plant species depends on the sugar concentration (and composition) of the nectar, on the accessibility of the nectar to the bees (fig. 12), and on other factors that have been discussed in Chapter 1. But, however good the nectar is from the bees' point of view, the plant species will yield a major amount of honey only if it flowers prolifically over a large area, and preferably for weeks rather than days.

HONEYDEW

The phloem sap which transports nutrients to the tissues of a plant is inaccessible to bees, unless it seeps out of a surface wound, under pressure from within. Some plant-sucking insects, belonging to the order Rhynchota, have mouthparts which can pierce plant surfaces, and the phloem sap is then forced out through the puncture by internal pressure, which is reinforced by the insect's own pumping. The sap passes from the mouthparts of the insect through its digestive tract, by one of two routes: either from foregut to midgut (where it is digested) to hindgut (where it is absorbed); or directly from foregut to hindgut through filter chambers, bypassing the midgut. This dual system allows the insect to cope with a large quantity of very dilute food – it may be as much as the insect's own weight every three hours (or for young larvae, very much more). The excess food is found on leaves, twigs, etc. in small droplets and is known as honeydew. It is collected by other insects including bees and ants.

Honeydew differs in its composition from phloem sap – and from nectar, which is wholly of plant origin – and honeydew honey has certain different characteristics from nectar honey. Honeydew contains enzymes derived from the secretions of the salivary glands and the gut of plant-sucking insects. The amount of nitrogen in honeydew ($0.2–1.0$ per cent of the dry matter) is much higher than in nectar, and $70–90$ per cent of it is in amino acids and amides. Honeydew also always contains organic acids, especially citric acid. But, as in nectar, carbohydrates comprise $90–95$ per cent of the solids, and in the main these consist of various sugars, often including some that are not present in the phloem sap but are synthesized during the passage through the insect, by the action of enzymes from the gut and the salivary glands. In certain cases there are sugar alcohols (dulcitol, sorbitol, inositol, ribitol), and sugar phosphates have occasionally been found. These contributions from the plant-sucking insects are carried over into the honey, and enable honeydew honey to be identified as such.

OTHER SOURCES OF HONEY

The raw materials of all honeys are derived from phloem sap, which flows through the soft tissues of plants. It is collected directly by bees in some circumstances. Cut sugar cane is the most common and prolific source. Bees have no piercing structure in their mouthparts, and their mandibles are not strong enough to cut a plant surface, so they cannot reach the sweet juices of fruits, as wasps can, except in one or two extremely soft-skinned varieties.

Bees will also collect sugary materials that are not nectar or other natural plant exudations if these happen to be available. Some curious examples are reported from time to time in beekeeping journals, for example pink 'honey' from a factory making raspberry jam; 'honey' from sugar-processing establishments; even chocolate 'honey' from a confectionery factory, and Coca-Cola 'honey' from used tins left by tourists at the Tower of London.

Since the generally agreed definition of honey states that it is produced from flower nectar or from other secretions from living plants, sugar fed to bees in their hive, in any form except honey itself, cannot be made into honey. The product may well be edible and wholesome, but it lacks many of the minor constituents that characterize honeys and give them their aroma and flavour.

In 1969–1970 we learned quite a lot about so-called 'sugar honey' through the following circumstances. In many countries sugar is sold at a subsidized price for feeding to colonies of bees in winter. To prevent misapplication of this concession, the sugar is denatured (made unsuitable for direct human consumption). For instance a little octosan may be added to it, which tastes bitter to man but not to bees. In autumn 1969, beekeepers in England were able to buy concessionary sugar syrup that had been marked with a green dye, and far more dye was used than was necessary. Syrup stored in the brood box in which the bees wintered was, not surprisingly, green. Next spring, when boxes of empty honey combs were put on the hives above the brood box in which the bees had wintered, beekeepers found that green 'honey' was stored in some of these combs. It was a clear demonstration that the bees had moved their stores around in the hive, emptying cells in the brood box in which the queen subsequently laid eggs. This experience showed beekeepers how careful they must be, in order to avoid labelling as 'honey' material the bees had not collected from living plants.

THE IMPORTANT HONEY PLANTS

In some regions of the world a crop that is a good honey plant – alfalfa, rape, or citrus, for instance – is grown over a large area of land, to the exclusion of all other plants. Single-source honey can be produced in such regions. But in most localities honey comes from various sources, and many English honeys are characterized by a great complexity of plant origins. A detailed study of one area was made by Dorothy Hodges in Surrey for 17 years, starting in 1940. Fig. 9 summarizes the situation; in any one year the flowering dates might be different from those shown, but they always followed the same sequence. Of the 105 plants worked by bees, 18 could be regarded as major honey plants, although several of these flower early and their honey would be used up by the bees in the spring when the colony is growing. This leaves as possible sources of honey for the beekeeper:

in May – dandelion, sycamore, hawthorn
in June – sainfoin, bean, raspberry
in June/July – white clover, blackberry, second-cut red clover
in July/August – willowherb, bell heather, lime
in August/September – ling heather, mustard.

Not more than three or four of these plants are likely to be present extensively in any one locality, and – in England at any rate – the weather may prevent bees flying during the flowering of one or more of them. So what the beekeeper harvests is only a fraction of what in theory might be available. This fraction is higher in regions where large areas are covered with good honey sources and where the climate is predictable, so that the beekeeper can foretell the date of each flow. The apparent busyness of a honeybee in a garden may be due less to the richness of the flow than to her need to visit many flowers in collecting one nectar load. Bees working a heavy flow are unmistakable: they fly from their hives like bullets, in the direction of the flowers that are yielding; if the flowers are tree-borne, then as you stand under the tree you hear the bees loud overhead. This is one of the happiest sounds a beekeeper knows.

We have so far considered a single locality. Multiply this by the number of such localities in the world, and it will come as no surprise that a detailed record of the world's honey sources has not yet been made. It would comprise a good proportion of the 250,000 flowering plants that exist. A shortlist of 232 plants, known to be major sources of honey on a world scale, is given in Appendix 2 (Table 1) with the continental distribution of each (Europe, Asia, Africa, the Americas, and Oceania). North and south temperate regions, and tropical areas, are differentiated.

From these and many tens of thousands of other plants, wild and cultivated, all the world's honey is produced. The sweetness of their nectars and the fragrance of their aromas are captured and preserved in this honey.

3. Constituents and characteristics of honey

The major components of honey are the sugars, of which the monosaccharides fructose and glucose together make up around 70 per cent of the total; disaccharides including sucrose add perhaps 10 per cent, and the water in which the sugars are dissolved 17–20 per cent. Yet many of the characteristics for which honey is well known – its flavour, aroma and colour for instance – are determined not by these major components but by others that are present in quite minute amounts. So far, 181 different substances have been identified in honey, some not known to exist elsewhere. In this chapter the various sugars are dealt with first, and then the minor constituents, some of which are also very important, are considered. The physical properties of honey, which depend on its constituents, are discussed next, and finally a method for identifying the plant sources of honeys. The exact composition of any one honey depends mainly on the plant sources it is derived from, but also on the weather, soil, and other factors, and no two honeys are identical. The infinite variety is in fact one of the great attractions of honey, and it can be appreciated best by those who harvest honey direct from the hive.

Appendix 2 (Table 4) sets out average and extreme percentages of the major constituents of honey mentioned above. The exceptionally high concentration of the sugars dissolved in the water was explained in Chapter 1. Honey is so supersaturated that if it is kept in a cool place the least soluble of the sugars starts to crystallize out, and the honey finally becomes granulated, but if granulated honey is warmed, the crystals re-dissolve and it becomes liquid again. Granulated honey is sometimes called *thick*, and liquid honey *clear*, but these terms are not precise enough to satisfy the honey specialist. The interplay between granulation and the composition – and hence the plant source – of honey is explained later in this chapter.

SUGARS AND THE SWEETNESS OF HONEY

The question 'What is sweeter than honey?' could receive the literal reply 'some other honeys'. All honey is sweet, since around 80 per cent of it consists of sugars, but some honeys taste sweeter than others because sugars differ in their sweetness. Some of the extra-sweet honeys are from acacia in south-east Europe; from sainfoin, *Onobrychis sativa*, like the famous *miel du Gâtinais* of central France; from thistles, *Cirsium* spp.; and from Himalayan balsam, *Impatiens glandulifera*. This last plant easily becomes naturalized in suitable damp places; it spread rapidly in the 1960s in Europe, and has been reported to yield up to 20 kg of honey per colony in England, Germany and Switzerland.

Both the total sugar content and the sugar composition of a specific honey influence its sweetness. Sweetness as assessed by human beings, which is important gastronomically, will be considered first; sweetness as assessed by bees is not necessarily the same, and does not have the same basis, but it is important in honey production.

The two main sugars of honey are fructose and glucose, in roughly equal proportions. Normally fructose predominates slightly, but there are exceptional honeys with more glucose than fructose – rape and dandelion are examples. Fructose is slightly sweeter than sucrose, glucose is rather less sweet, and maltose, another disaccharide in honey, is less sweet still. The enhanced sweetness of honeys in general is due to their high fructose content, and many extra-sweet honeys contain more than the average amount of fructose, but this is not the whole story.

We assess sweetness subjectively, and different individuals may react differently. Moreover the relative sweetness of different sugars is not the same at all concentrations: dilute solutions of sucrose (up to 10 per cent) taste sweeter than the corresponding solution of invert sugar (glucose + fructose), but as the concentration increases the sweetness of sucrose lags more and more behind that of its equivalent glucose + fructose mixture.

In 1976 the journal *Gleanings in Bee Culture* (p. 266) reported how a tasting panel of eleven students in the USA rated ten honeys for sweetness. Their rating for each honey type was compared with the sweetness calculated from sugar analysis of the same honey type, using the sweetness factors sucrose = 100, fructose = 175, glucose = 66, maltose = 30, and adding the contributions from the separate sugars. The average ratings by taste were fairly close in rank to those calculated, although there were some unexplained individual variations.

Many mixtures of sugars taste sweeter than would be expected by adding their separate effects together. A possible mechanism for this may be one of timing: the sweetness of sucrose is perceived more quickly than that of glucose, so in a mixture the slower-acting glucose exerts its maximum effect after the sucrose effect has worn off.

Bees' order of preference for sugar solutions has been reported as: sucrose, glucose, maltose, fructose, but it probably varies with concentration. Assuming that sweetness is the factor that attracts bees to drink the sugar solutions, bees may be more sensitive than man to the composition of sugar mixtures, and less sensitive to total sugar concentration. But they are well able to identify (and collect) nectar with a high sugar concentration when a choice is available. Nectar can vary between 3 per cent and 87 per cent sugar, but many nectars contain around 30–40 per cent.

A complete list of sugars in honey is given in Appendix 2 (Table 5). The whole subject of sugar analysis and identification is complex, and we shall not pursue it here. It is now known that many results reported before 1950, and some even into the 1960s, are not valid.

The most important group of constituents of honey, after the monosaccharides (glucose and fructose) and sucrose, are the reducing disaccharides (maltose, etc.). As a result of enzyme activity their amount seems to increase during storage, depending on storage conditions. One honey sample kept for 36 years was reported to contain 16 per cent of maltose and related compounds.

The shelf-life of honey is sometimes quoted commercially as $2\frac{1}{2}$ years, but honey does not 'go bad' as many foods do; it is still wholesome after decades. In 1977 I had occasion to inspect and taste over a hundred samples of honey from different countries that had been stored for 20–25 years. None had suffered active spoilage, but the fine flavours that characterized many of the honeys had gone, and what was left was nondescript sweetness, less than that of fresh honey because of the greater proportion of maltose. Strong honey flavours tend to survive longest. My last crop of heather honey was harvested on the North Yorkshire moors in 1954; we have used it for more than twenty years, although latterly it has been relegated to cooking rather than table use. Honey has been recovered in the Arctic from stores left by other much earlier expeditions. The oldest honey I have seen is in the Agricultural Museum at Dokki in Egypt, where two honey pots from New Kingdom tombs (*c.* 1400 BC) still have their contents in them.

It is important to store honey under suitable conditions. If honey is not kept sealed it can deteriorate through fermentation; if it is stored at high temperatures – especially in contact with ferrous metals, for instance where their galvanized or tin coating is damaged – honey can deteriorate through abnormal chemical reactions.

THE AROMAS AND FLAVOURS OF HONEY

Apart from its sweetness, the flavour of honey is closely related to its aroma, and both these characteristics depend on minute amounts of complex substances in the honey, derived from its plant sources. Different honeys therefore have different aromas and flavours; an expert can detect many single-source honeys by smelling and tasting them, and he can make a good guess at the main plant contributors to honeys from mixed sources. Some aromas and flavours are, however, so dominant that they mask any others in the same honey. My heather honey still fills the house with a splendid and recognizable aroma when it is used for cooking, even after twenty years' storage.

The greatest experts are probably those employed as honey tasters in honey-importing firms and in processing and packing plants where a true assessment of plant origin is of economic importance. Beekeepers who serve as judges at honey shows learn to recognize many honeys produced in their own country from aroma and flavour alone – and as a rule no other test is applied to

13. This 1788 honey advertisement shows a nice appreciation of different honeys. The caption reads: Richd Hoy, At his Honey-Warehouse N° 175, Piccadilly Sells the choicest & purest Honey only, Fine Minorca Honey, D.° Narbone Honey, D.° Breakfast Honey, D.° Honey Comb, Box and Glass Bee-hives contrived so as Ladies may have them on their dressing Tables, without the least danger of being stung.

confirm or refute their opinion. Ten fairly widely available honeys, that readers could well learn to identify by aroma and flavour, are:

acacia from Hungary and Romania
rape from the widely grown oilseed crop
rosemary from the Mediterranean area
orange blossom from Spain, USA, Israel
lime, basswood from Europe, North America
sweet chestnut widespread in Europe
thyme from Greece; 'Hymettus' honey was probably a mixture
    of thyme with savory, *Satureia*, and marjoram, *Origanum*
eucalyptus exported from Australia, but produced in many
    areas elsewhere; individual *Eucalyptus* honeys vary widely
bell heather, *Erica cinerea*   ⎱ both from the seaboard of
ling heather, *Calluna vulgaris* ⎰ western Europe.

Milder, water-white honeys (each with a distinctive flavour) are placed first above, and darker, more strongly flavoured and aromatic ones last; the link between flavour and colour will be discussed later.

Subjectively assessed and described aromas or flavours are of little use for comparative purposes except with a single operator. Even the vocabulary of descriptive words is very small and inadequate. The journal *Language* recently reported of wine experts: 'Some said "light" when others said "full-bodied"; some said "withered" when others thought a wine "full of character". The only thing they agreed upon was that the wines they liked were "dry", and wines they didn't like tended to be "sweet". But this was irrespective of sugar content.' Some similar comments could be made about honey.

Chemical identification of the individual substances contributing to the flavour of different honeys is very difficult. Apart from the sugars, these compounds include amino and other acids (especially gluconic); proline; tannins; glucosidic and alkaloidal compounds; also, specifically, diacetyl (or other diketoalkane) in heather honey, and methyl anthranilate in orange honey.

In general the most pleasing aroma components of honey are those with low boiling points, which are the most evanescent. So the aroma and flavour are at their best when the honey is taken straight from the hive. They may be changed slightly even by spinning the honey out of the combs in a centrifugal extractor, which exposes a large surface of it to the atmosphere. The 1976 *Australian Bee Journal* reported the experimental use of baffles in a centrifuge to reduce the distance through which the fine streams of honey are thrown through the air. Components with higher boiling points – including HMF (hydroxymethylfurfural) – seem to be responsible for the characteristic honey aroma in general.

Although honey is remarkably resistant to major change or deterioration, every treatment or exposure it receives is likely to bring about subtle changes that slightly reduce its interest from a gastronomic point of view. Appendix 2 (Table 6) gives a full up-to-date list of aroma constituents identified in honey.

THE COLOUR OF HONEY

'Honey-coloured' is usually interpreted as something darker than cream and lighter than brown, with a sort of richness and pleasantness about it. The colour of liquid honey can in fact range from water-white to nearly black, with variants towards tints of green or red, or even blue. Water-white honeys come from rape, sage, acacia, and red clover. Pearly white honey is produced from *Ipomoea*, known as campanilla or morning glory; light golden honey from viper's bugloss, *Echium*; deep golden yellow honey from golden rod, *Solidago*; and intense golden yellow from dandelion. Of more unusual colours, there is greyish-yellow honey from borage, greenish honey from lime (linden or basswood) and greenish brown from tree of heaven, *Ailanthus altissima*, and maple. Darker honeys include port wine colours from various heaths, *Erica*, dark or reddish brown from ling heather, and dark brown from tamarisk.

On the world market honey is graded by its colour, light honeys commanding a higher price than dark honeys. The flavour and aroma of honeys, as of any other foodstuff, are more important than its colour, but they are very much more difficult than colour to assess quantitatively. There is a rough and ready connection between colour and flavour, in that honeys with a delicate flavour are always light, whereas dark honeys normally have a strong flavour. But there are also some light honeys with a strong flavour.

Countries with a long tradition of high honey consumption used to produce much honey that had a light colour and mild flavour. When these countries started to import large amounts of honey in modern times, their preference influenced the price structure, and they sought light honeys similar to their home-produced honey. Colour assessment was used as a convenient flavour indicator, and higher prices were therefore paid for light honeys.

Colour can be a reliable indicator of honey quality in one respect. Honey becomes darker during storage, more rapidly at higher temperatures, and darkening can be especially hastened by temperatures high enough to damage the honey. Contamination with metals also darkens honey. Nevertheless some honeys are dark when freshly made by the bees, and different honeys darken at different rates, even under the same conditions.

When empty light-coloured combs, and empty combs darkened from brood rearing, were inserted alternately in hives, it was found that the brooded combs darkened the honey stored in them. Their use is thus a practice to be avoided by beekeepers – as it usually is, on hygienic grounds.

Colour descriptions are rather less subjective than aroma and flavour descriptions, and they can be made objective (see below), although very often they are not. In particular, a medium-coloured, medium-flavoured honey might be described as rather dark and strong-flavoured by a Canadian who is used to white bland honey, or as rather pale and flavourless by an Australian used to dark honey with a fairly pronounced flavour.

The colour of honey offered for sale is commonly described in terms that are more imaginative and attractive than those used by technicians trying to compare a large number of honeys for matching purposes. The standard commercial apparatus for measuring and classifying honey colour is the Pfund colour grader, manufactured by the Koehler Manufacturing Company in the USA. It is calibrated against glass colour standards for honey that were developed in 1956. The Pfund grader consists of a standard amber glass wedge, with which the liquid honey is compared visually, the honey being contained in a wedge-shaped cell. The lightness or darkness of the honey is expressed by the distance in millimetres on a scale along the amber wedge, whose scale is subdivided into honey 'colours'. Unfortunately, the name of the colour for any particular distance along the wedge is not the same for all countries; Appendix 2 (Table 7) gives details. In the United Kingdom, colours of honey for sale are categorized as Select Light Colour, Select Medium Colour, or Select Dark Colour, as determined by 'standard' colour glasses, not by reference to the Pfund scale.

Colours of honey and their descriptions have thus already been standardized in various individual countries for industrial use, and it would be a great step forward if one set of standards could be used throughout the world for describing honeys, with agreed translations in different languages. At present no one really knows what someone else means by a colour description of honey, unless the colour is one of those that can be defined by Pfund colour-class boundaries – and these are limited to a single sequence of colours, each darker than the previous one.

In the modern honey industry colour has an intrinsic importance in helping large-scale packers to put out a standardized blended product from year to year, and all through the year. Either Pfund reading or optical density can be used in honey blending for direct determination of the quantities of different honeys needed to obtain a specified colour grade. Optical density (degree of opaqueness, non-transparency) is a quantitative characteristic of honey, and can be more useful than the Pfund reading (see Appendix 2, Table 7).

Honey appears lighter in colour after it has granulated; this is due partly to the transparency of liquid honey and the opacity of granulated honey. Only a very thin layer of granulated honey can be seen at once, and a layer of liquid honey of this thickness would also look much lighter than a jarful. The colour of any one sample of honey when it granulates depends on the crystal size; the finest crystals give the lightest appearance.

The substances responsible for the colour of honey are still largely unknown. Minerals are among the factors believed to be responsible and these are discussed later.

Honeys usually become darker as a result of storage, although at widely differing rates, depending on their composition (acidity, nitrogen and fructose contents) and their initial colour. Any previous darkening due to processing is likely to be followed by less darkening during subsequent storage. Individual honeys can vary widely in their rate of darkening during storage, even without previous processing. This darkening is temperature-sensitive; it may well be linked directly or indirectly with production of HMF, discussed later.

ENZYMES IN HONEY

In discussing the aroma, flavour and colour of honey, we were dealing with minute quantities of substances about which rather little is known. The enzymes – also present in minute quantities – are known and identified, but their action has not yet been completely unravelled. There are three important enzymes in honey: invertase, diastase (amylase), and glucose oxidase. Others, including catalase and acid phosphatase, may also be present.

Enzymes are among the most interesting components of honey, not because they have nutritional significance in human diet, but because they play a vital part in the production of honey from its raw plant materials. The conversion of nectar or honeydew into honey can be brought about only by the action of certain enzymes, and these are present in glandular secretions of the bees.

Invertase, produced by the bees' hypopharyngeal glands, 'inverts' the sucrose from the plant into glucose + fructose. (The plant raw materials of honey – especially honeydew – may themselves also have invertase activity, but the latest research rejects the suggestion that they make any contribution to honey invertase.) Some invertase is still present in the finished honey, with the result that the inversion may be carried further after the honey is extracted from the combs and during storage. Invertase is, however, inactivated by heating (see Appendix 2, Table 8).

Diastase (amylase), another enzyme occurring in honey, is produced by the bees' hypopharyngeal glands and also occurs in plants. It breaks down starch, and may be involved in the bees' digestion of pollen. Its main relevance to honey is that it is even more sensitive to heat than invertase, and that this property led the German honey industry to regard a low level of diastase in honey as an indication that the honey had been overheated. Some exporting countries object to this, since fresh honeys from different plant sources, and gathered under different conditions, differ much in their enzyme contents. For instance honeys from orange and other citrus, and from some eucalypts, can contain less diastase than the permitted German minimum, even when taken from the hive.

In general, honeys from very rapid flows, when the colonies have much incoming nectar to process, have lower enzyme levels than those from less rich flows, which the bees have time to process intensively. Similarly nectars with a high sugar content need less manipulation to convert them into honey than more dilute nectars, and so honeys from concentrated nectars tend to have low invertase and diastase levels. (On the other hand 'honey' made by bees from dry sugar fed to them has a high enzyme content, because the bees must moisten and dilute the sugar before they can take it into the hive and store it.) In the nature of things heavy flows are more common in honey-exporting than in honey-importing countries – where honey standards were set early in the history of the world honey trade. One aim of these standards was to detect adulteration of imported honey with industrial sugars.

A theoretical argument against the use of diastase level in

assessing honey quality is that it implies that the diastase (or invertase) has some special nutritional value in itself, although the function of enzymes is in the production of honey, which could not occur without them.

Another enzyme in honey that originates in the secretion of the bees' hypopharyngeal glands is glucose oxidase. Like invertase and diastase it plays a part in the elaboration of honey in the hive; it oxidizes glucose in the unripened honey, which still has a high water content. It is virtually inactive in full-density honey, but becomes active again in diluted honey, producing gluconic acid and hydrogen peroxide. It is sensitive to visible light as well as to heat. Substances found in honey, reported in the 1930s, which appeared to inhibit bacterial growth and were called 'inhibines', were shown in the 1960s to be due to the presence and action of glucose oxidase.

Two other enzymes that have been reported in honey are catalase and acid phosphatase. In so far as they occur, it seems likely that they are of plant origin, and they are not known to be important in the elaboration of honey.

OTHER SUBSTANCES IN HONEY

Honey contains acids (the average pH is about 3·9), which contribute to its resistance to damage by micro-organisms. The tartness they produce also enhances its flavour. Honey contains much more gluconic acid than any other acid; it is produced by the action on glucose of the enzyme glucose oxidase from the bees' hypopharyngeal glands. All the other acids are present in much smaller quantities, and their sources are not known; some may occur in nectar. An old belief, not founded on fact, was that the bees add formic acid to the honey in order to preserve it – even injecting it from the sting into each cell. Formic acid is only one of a number of acids that have been identified with certainty in honey; others are: acetic, benzoic, butyric, citric, *iso*valeric, lactic, maleic, malic, oxalic, phenylacetic, propionic, pyroglutamic, succinic, valeric.

As well as these acids, honey also contains amino acids. Proline is by far the most important of these, then come lysine, glutamic acid and aspartic acid. Others are: alanine, arginine, cystine, glycine, histidine, *iso*leucine, leucine, methionine, phenylalanine, serine, threonine, tryptophan, tyrosine, valine. In general, the greatest significance of the amino acids is that they can provide 'finger prints' distinguishing one type of honey from another, and honeys *per se* from synthetic substances masquerading as honey.

Amino acids are breakdown products of proteins which, in normal honeys, also exist in no more than minute amounts, contributed by the bees rather than by the plant, and insignificant from a dietary viewpoint. A few honeys, however, contain proteins from the plant of origin, giving the honey abnormal properties, including a gel-like consistency which is discussed with the flow properties of honey. The first such honey to be investigated was from ling heather.

Buckwheat honey, *Fagopyrum esculentum*, contains colloidal material, in which two proteins have been found with molecular weights about 146,000 and 73,000. In various other honeys, molecular weights for proteins of plant origin have been reported as 98,000 and 400,000; for proteins of bee origin as 40,000 and 240,000.

Honey also contains minute amounts of many different minerals which originate in the plants, and hence vary in different honeys. Minerals are among the many components that affect honey colour. Very light-coloured honeys often contain little mineral matter, and dark honeys may well contain much – although not necessarily, since the colour also depends on other factors.

The total weight of the mineral elements (total ash) varies from say 0·02 per cent to 1·0 per cent of the honey; it is commonly 0·1 per cent to 0·3 per cent. The following honeys often contain less than 0·1 per cent of minerals, i.e. unusually little:

　　water-white and very light: lucerne, sainfoin, rape, acacia
　　light and light amber: tree fruit, white clover, rosemary
　　light, somewhat greenish: lime
　　dark: buckwheat.

Dark honeys that have high mineral contents include ling heather and, especially, honeydew honey. A very high mineral content (1 per cent) is in fact likely to be found only in honeydew honey, and can thus be used as an indicator of such honeys.

Honey contains much more potassium than any other mineral,

100 times as much as iron, for instance. Appendix 2 lists 28 minerals that have been identified in honey (Table 9) and compares their amounts with the amounts that should be contained in our diet (Table 13).

Calcium oxalate crystals have been found in honeys that come entirely from lime, sweet chestnut and mint, and they also have been identified in the nectars of these plants.

Perhaps the most discussed minor constituent of honey is hydroxymethylfurfural, commonly referred to as HMF. This compound results from the breakdown of hexose sugars such as glucose and fructose in the presence of an acid, and it has assumed importance in honey quality control because the amount of it in a honey sample is used as an indirect indicator of quality.

The amount of HMF certainly increases in honeys subjected to high temperatures. Every extra 10°C (18°F) speeds up HMF production about $4\frac{1}{2}$ times; for example an increase taking 100 days at 30°C (86°F) takes about 20 days at 40°C (104°F), 4 days at 50°C (122°F), 1 day at 60°C (140°F) and only a few hours at 70°C (158°F).

The EEC recommended upper limit for HMF is 40 ppm. Honeys with much lower HMF levels have almost certainly not been overheated, and honeys from sources common in Western Europe that have considerably higher HMF levels probably have been overheated or mistreated in some other way. But natural HMF levels in some of the world's honeys, produced under climatic conditions unknown in Europe, are above the limit acceptable to the EEC. In tropical climates, the temperatures in the hive may be high, and honey that is left in the hive after the flow may develop a high HMF level. It is certainly natural honey, although one might say it is spoilt natural honey. A similar argument may be relevant to enzymes.

The following vitamins have so far been identified in honey: vitamin B_1 (thiamine); vitamin B_2 complex: riboflavin, nicotinic acid (niacin), B_6 (pyridoxine), pantothenic acid; and vitamin C (ascorbic acid). Their presence in honey is interesting, though the amounts are too small to be of nutritional significance. Vitamin C occurs in occasional nectars, notably the mint *Mentha aquatica*.

A few honeys, and the nectar or honeydew they are derived from, are toxic to man. One early case of honey poisoning was described by Xenophon in his *Anabasis*. In 400 BC Xenophon's army was not far from Trebizond (Trabzon) on the Black Sea:

> The Greeks ascended the mountain and camped in a number of villages which were well stocked with food. There was nothing remarkable about them, except that there were great numbers of bee hives in these parts, and all the soldiers who ate the honey went off their heads and suffered from vomiting and diarrhoea and were unable to stand upright. Those who had only eaten a little behaved as though they were drunk, and those who had eaten a lot were like mad people. So there were numbers of them lying on the ground, as though after a defeat, and there was a general state of despondency. However, they were all alive on the next day, and came to themselves at about the same hour as they had eaten the honey the day before. On the third and fourth days they were able to get up, and felt just as if they had been taking medicine (purgative). (Xenophon, *The Persian Expedition*, trans. Rex Warner, Penguin 1949, p. 169.)

The honey in question was from *Rhododendron ponticum*, and most other known toxic honeys are from members of the same family, Ericaceae (*Azalea, Andromeda, Kalmia*). In New Zealand, cases of poisoning from honey in the 1940s led to the identification of a new compound, christened mellitoxin, in honey from the tree *Coriaria arborea*. It was not the nectar that was toxic, nor the honey produced when the plant was in flower, but honeydew on the leaves, secreted by the insect *Scolypopa australis*.

Toxic honey is hardly a problem that need concern the consumer, since toxicity is very rare, and the plants in question are known, and avoided, by honey producers. In any case when the honey is ripe any toxic substances have usually disappeared; one suspects that Xenophon's soldiers took unripe honey combs from the hives.

A few pollens are poisonous to bees, and also a few nectars, but these will not normally be made into honey. On the other hand improperly applied pesticides, especially the systemics that enter the fluid system of a plant, can contaminate the nectar and pollen of flowers, and many bees are poisoned and killed by them each year.

In dry years large numbers of dead or paralysed bees may be found under flowering lime trees. The poisoning is due not to toxic alkaloids such as occur in many poisonous plants, but to unusual sugars in lime nectar and pollen, which disturb the carbohydrate metabolism of the bees. Mannose is the chief of these sugars. Bees have only a negligible amount of the enzyme that hydrolyses (breaks down) mannose, and they are therefore unable to digest it. But they have a large amount of the enzyme that phosphorylates mannose (combines it with phosphoric acid). In bees that eat pollen or nectar containing mannose, a toxic compound mannose-6-phosphate accumulates, and the presence of mannose also prevents the normal assimilation of glucose and fructose. Even hydrolysates of lime pollen and nectar are poisonous to bees. The mannose compound in the blood and in the thorax prevents movement of the wings and legs by the thoracic muscles, and hence paralyses the bees – temporarily or permanently. *Tilia petiolaris, Tilia tomentosa* and *Tilia orbicularis* seem to be the species most implicated, and wild bees to be more affected than honeybees – although there is one Swiss report of 50 per cent of the foraging bees from an apiary dying from this cause.

This ends the catalogue of substances in honeys, except for microscopic constituents in suspension (yeasts, also pollen grains in honey from flowers, and algae and moulds in honeydew honey) but before dealing with them we must consider the physical properties of honey.

GRANULATION OF HONEY

The physical and physicochemical properties of honey are governed by the constituents already discussed. Several of these properties are of the greatest economic importance in the honey industry, for reasons that will be seen; all of them are much more complex than the accounts given here might seem to indicate.

All honeys are liquid when produced by bees; they are supersaturated solutions, at any rate at storage or room temperatures, which are 10°–20°C (18°–36°F) below hive temperatures, and crystallization (granulation) is quite likely to start within some weeks or months (more rarely within days or years). The first sugar to crystallize out of solution is glucose, and of the various indexes to the granulating tendency of different honeys that have been devised and tested, the most useful is the ratio between the glucose content and the water content of each honey (Appendix 2, Table 10). An index used earlier, and still often referred to, was the ratio between the fructose (laevulose) and glucose (dextrose) contents (L/D); if this was above 2 the honey was regarded as safe from granulation. But this takes no account of the amount of water in the honey, in which both the sugars are dissolved. Honeys with less than 17 per cent water are more likely to granulate than those with 18 per cent; those with more than 19 per cent may well be in danger of fermentation. Honeys containing less than 30 per cent glucose rarely if ever granulate.

Apart from the sugar composition of honey, the course of granulation depends largely on the presence or absence of minute suspended particles that can serve as nuclei for crystal growth. Such nuclei normally exist even in clear liquid honey, although they are invisible to the naked eye: minute crystals, air bubbles, beeswax particles, pollen grains, dust from the air or the honey container.

Commercially, honey to be sold liquid is processed by flash heating to 60°–71°C (140°–160°F), which dissolves any crystals and helps to expel incorporated air, and then by filtering under pressure through diatomaceous earth, to remove all or most of the solid particles – including those that occur naturally in the honey. According to one school of thought, this removal of natural constituents is as unacceptable as the introduction of additives. The removal of pollen grains certainly prevents their use to determine the plant origin of the honey. Such commercial processing is in any case outside the reach of the domestic producer.

Honeys with a low glucose/water ratio are likely to remain liquid with no special treatment; such non-granulating honeys include acacia, tupelo, *Nyssa aquatica*, and milkweed, *Asclepias*. Honeys with a high glucose/water ratio fairly quickly become completely granulated and should be sold after this has occurred; examples are rape, dandelion and tah, *Viguiera helianthoides*. Rapid crystallization normally produces a fine granulation, and this gives the product a pleasant consistency.

The majority of honeys are intermediate between the above extremes, and they are likely to start to granulate during storage – whether before selling, or in the shop, or in the home. In so far as they granulate evenly, before they are sold, they do not present any difficulty, because they will be sold as granulated honey. But some of these honeys may granulate unevenly; a layer of crystals is overlaid by a layer of liquid with a higher water content, in which fermentation may start; even if not, the separated honey looks unattractive, and is not very nice to eat. The easiest solution to the problem is to induce fine granulation by providing nuclei for crystals to grow on; a small amount of honey already finely granulated, usually from last year's crop, is stirred into the new honey.

Each capped cell of the comb provides an environment for honey storage that is protected from moisture, dust and other contaminants, and from adventitious crystals from round about. All this helps to inhibit granulation of honey in the comb. Nevertheless a few honeys (rape is an example) may granulate in the comb if the beekeeper does not remove and extract his crop promptly.

DENSITY, WATER CONTENT, FERMENTATION, HYGROSCOPICITY

Honey has a higher density than almost any other foodstuff – nearly 50 per cent higher than the density of water. Honey therefore occupies not much more than two-thirds as much space as the same weight of water. More precisely, the relative density of honey is between 1·40 and 1·44 at 20°C (68°F), depending on its water content. Measurement of the relative density of a honey sample provides an easy way of assessing the water content of the honey. A suitable hydrometer can be used, or the refractive index can be measured with a refractometer, and a conversion table used (Appendix 2, Table 11).

The water content of honey, together with the number of yeast cells in it, determine whether and when the honey will ferment at a given temperature. All natural honeys contain sugar-tolerant yeasts, of which seven species of *Zygosaccharomyces* have been identified, two of *Saccharomyces*, and one each of *Nematospora*, *Schizosaccharomyces*, *Schwanniomyces* and *Torula*. Nectar and honeydew contain yeasts, and others may come from the body of the bee, the soil round the hive, and honey-house air and equipment.

Fermentation of honey (except in the preparation of alcoholic drinks, dealt with in Chapter 4) is wholly undesirable. A high total sugar content with a correspondingly low water content is the best insurance against fermentation. The highest safe water content is probably 19 per cent; if it is as low as 17 per cent fermentation would not occur even if many yeast cells are present. At 18 per cent several hundred yeast cells per gram might be permissible. Only sugar-tolerant yeasts, especially species of *Zygosaccharomyces*, are able to multiply in honey.

Because it is a highly concentrated sugar solution, honey is remarkably hygroscopic for a natural product: it absorbs water very readily under certain conditions. This can be a disadvantage, since the honey is then more liable to fermentation, but it can also be used to advantage, in that honey can impart the desirable property of softness or non-drying to food products in which it is incorporated; some recipes are given in Chapter 4. Whether or not any one honey will absorb water if left exposed to the air depends on its own water content and the extent to which the air is saturated with water vapour. If the relative humidity of the air (RH) is 60 per cent, honeys containing less than 18·3 per cent water will absorb water and those with more than 18·3 per cent water will lose water to the air. A useful set of such equilibrium values is:

RH of air %	50	55	60	65	70	75	80
% water in honey	15·9	16·8	18·3	20·9	24·2	28·3	33·1

The relative humidity of the air is reduced if the air is heated, and most honey handling is done in a warm atmosphere. But in a damp climate honey left unsealed in a cool place will soon become runny.

Bearing in mind both fermentation and, if the honey is liquid, unwanted granulation, storage temperatures for honey have the following advantages and disadvantages. Storage at 0°C (32°F) is too expensive in most honey-producing areas, but five weeks at 0°C can prevent subsequent granulation. Any temperature below 10°C (50°F) greatly retards granulation, and any up to 11°C (52°F) also discourages fermentation. But 11°–21°C (52°–70°F) is the range most likely to lead to fermentation, and 10°–18°C

(50°–64°F) the range most favourable for granulation, especially 14°C (57°F). Temperatures of 21°–27°C (70°–81°F) are less likely to lead to both fermentation and granulation, but enzymes are destroyed and HMF is produced rapidly, and the honey becomes darker. Above 27°C (81°F) there is no fermentation, but spoilage is even more rapid. On balance, honey should thus be stored at temperatures as low as is practicable, and if possible at or below 11°C (52°F).

FLOW PROPERTIES OF HONEY

When a normal Newtonian liquid is flowing, it is subject to internal friction, characterized by the viscosity of the liquid. Honeys with a high viscosity flow slowly, and do not for instance ooze off the bread they are spread on. They are sometimes described as being 'heavy-bodied', or having a 'good body', or even as having a 'good density', although their density is a different characteristic. Low-viscosity honeys are 'thin' or 'thin-bodied'; they are inconvenient for use as table honeys.

The viscosity of a honey depends largely on its water content, and is thus linked with its relative density; the less water, the higher the density and the viscosity.

There is a thirty-fold difference between the ease with which honeys flow, over the range of water contents that occur naturally. Honey becomes very much less viscous as the temperature rises; for instance it may flow 3 times as rapidly at a temperature only 7°C (13°F) higher. Appendix 2 (Table 12) gives the actual figures.

The speed of flow, and hence the viscosity, is of prime importance in the design and operation of honey piping systems, for instance in processing or bottling plants. It is easy to see that there can be a temptation to heat honey overmuch, in order to move it rapidly through a system; a far better method is to increase the pump capacity and pipe diameters instead.

A few honeys have abnormal (non-Newtonian) flow properties. For instance ling heather honey is well known for its gel-like consistency: it will not flow sufficiently for a centrifugal extractor to remove the honey from the cells. If the honey is agitated, it becomes more liquid and will flow. This property, known as thixotropy, is due to the relatively high content of certain proteins in the honey; if the proteins are removed and added to another honey, the thixotropic character is transferred with them. Other honeys that are thixotropic, by reason of their protein content, are manuka, *Leptospermum scoparium*, from New Zealand, and karvi, *Carvia callosa*, from India.

OTHER PROPERTIES OF HONEY

Several optical properties of honey are of practical importance. The *refractive index* increases with the content of solids, i.e. it decreases at higher water contents, and the use of a pocket refractometer provides an easy way of estimating the water content of honey. It is astonishing that many honey judges should still confine themselves to subjective assessments, when one of the basic quality characteristics of honey can so easily be measured objectively.

When polarized light passes through honey, the plane of polarization is shifted either clockwise or anticlockwise, according to the different sugars in it; this property is referred to as optical rotation. Glucose rotates the plane clockwise ($+$) and is called dextrorotatory; fructose rotates it anticlockwise ($-$) and is called laevorotatory: hence the alternative names for these sugars, dextrose and laevulose. Since most honeys from nectar contain more fructose than glucose, they have a negative specific rotation. Honeys from honeydew, with less fructose, and also adulterated honeys, usually have a positive specific rotation. So optical rotation has a diagnostic value. Honey also shows *mutarotation* – changes in the specific rotation linked with sugar changes, but not in a way that is straightforward, or indeed yet understood. *Optical density* was referred to in connection with the colour of honey.

Several thermal properties of honey also have a practical significance. The *calorific value* denotes the energy produced by its metabolism (in the bee, in man, or in any other organism). The *specific heat* governs the 'buffering action' of the honey stores in a hive against temperature fluctuations, which is important in winter for the bees clustered beneath the honey stores. At low temperatures honey is so viscous that it behaves more like a solid than a liquid, and its *thermal conductivity* is a major factor in determining the rate at which the honey in the centre of a large container becomes warm when heat is applied through the container walls; at high temperatures convection is the chief factor in heat transfer.

The calorific value of honey is usually quoted as 3·04 kcal/g (1380 kcal/lb). The specific heat of liquid honey is around 0·6, and of granulated honey somewhat higher. The thermal conductivity of honey increases with temperature and decreases with water content; for instance honey containing 15 per cent water has a thermal conductivity of 123 at 2°C and 143 at 71°C; for honey containing 21 per cent water the figures are 118 and 138 respectively (all $\times$ 10^{-5} cal/cm sec °C).

Honey lowers the freezing point of water in which it is dissolved: 15 per cent honey by 1·4°–1·5°C (2·5°–2·7°F), 68 per cent honey by 12°C (22°F).

The only electrical property of honey that need be considered here is its *electrical conductivity*, which has diagnostic value in indicating the source of the honey: whether nectar (with some differentiation according to species) or honeydew, and probably also whether adulterated. Electrical conductivity is usually measured on diluted honey; tests with 20% solutions gave values (all $\times$ 10^{-4}/ohm cm): 0·8 to 8·5 for flower honeys (heather honey 7·7), and 6·3 to 16·4 for honeydew honeys. Its measurement may possibly provide a rapid method for establishing whether or not honey is suitable for bees' winter stores, since some of the constituents that increase the conductivity also make honey unsuitable for bees confined to their hives by cold weather.

IDENTIFICATION OF PLANT SOURCES OF HONEYS BY POLLEN ANALYSIS

Some honeys can be identified with more or less certainty by their aroma (ling heather), colour (buckwheat), rapid crystallization (rape), flavour (leatherwood), or by a combination of these and other characteristics. Some honeys can be named because they are produced in hives situated within large tracts of one plant species during its flowering period: examples are lucerne in the USA, acacia in Hungary and Romania, individual species of eucalypt in Australia, lime in Poland, honeydew in the Black Forest of Germany. In areas with large-scale agriculture, and geological formations on a grand scale with large homogeneous areas of natural vegetation, there may be little doubt as to the source of honey obtained. This is especially true if the beekeeper is a good observer of his bees and of the plants within their foraging range.

It is, however, often very easy to make a wrong identification of the plant source of honey, either through lack of observation or knowledge, or through wishful thinking. For instance dandelion nectar has a higher sugar concentration than the nectars of many fruit trees, and may well contribute a higher proportion of 'tree' honey than is supposed. 'Citrus honey' and 'orange honey' are useful descriptions for marketing the harvest from hives near citrus groves, but who is to tell how much of the honey is derived from citrus and how much from other plants in flower at the time? Heather honey has a very strong, characteristic flavour and aroma, which will be manifest even if half the honey has come from plants that bloomed before the heather flowers opened.

In parts of the world with a very mixed agriculture, and an intimately varied tapestry of trees, shrubs and ground plants, it may be difficult even to guess what plants have contributed most to any one crop of honey. It is, I think, no accident that methods for the pollen analysis of honey were developed in Western Europe, and especially in countries with a small-scale pattern of vegetation such as Germany and Switzerland.

Pollen is collected by bees, and is carried to the hive on their hind legs (fig. 1); the bees 'handle' it separately from honey, and store it in different cells. Nevertheless a few grains of pollen from a flower may find their way into its nectar, and some may also get into the nectar via the hairs of a bee's body, and in other ways; so honey itself usually contains pollen grains from the flowers that have contributed their nectar to it. (Honeydew contributes its own tell-tale microscopic components, listed at the end of this section.)

Pollen grains of different plants can be distinguished under a microscope by their size and shape, and their surface patterns of furrows, pores, spines, etc. The study of pollen grains is known as palynology, and hence the study of pollen grains in honey as

61

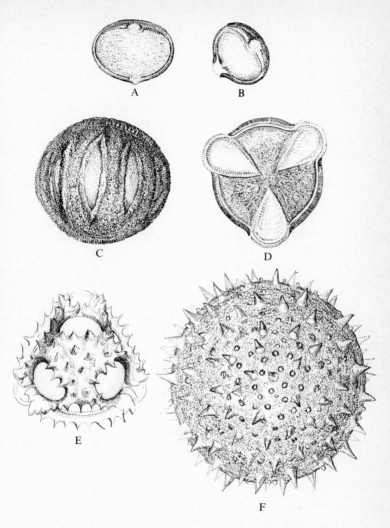

14. Pollen grains, 1,000–1,300 times their natural size (except F, 450 times):

A   bird's-foot trefoil, *Lotus corniculatus*   Leguminosae
B   Spanish chestnut, *Castanea sativa*   Fagaceae
C   borage, *Borago officinalis*   Boraginaceae
D   sycamore, *Acer pseudoplatanus*   Aceraceae
E   dandelion, *Taraxacum officinale*   Compositae
F   hollyhock, *Althaea rosea*   Malvaceae

melissopalynology. Identification of the different pollen grains is based on expert knowledge and on constant reference to a set of microscope slides carrying suitably prepared grains of pollen collected directly from individual plant species. Photomicrographs of these and other pollen grains can usefully enlarge such a reference collection.

In the 1920s and 1930s, when the pollen analysis of honey was being established on a competent basis, photographic film and equipment were much less advanced than now, and drawings of the pollen grains were of great importance for reference. The English artist Dorothy Hodges reached an unprecedented standard in her series of drawings of pollen grains as she saw them under her microscope. Six of her previously unpublished drawings, all except one representing important world honey plants, are reproduced in fig. 14. Pollen grains of plants belonging to the same family may show similar characteristics, and some families are characterized by extraordinarily intricate and beautiful pollens, for instance Compositae (E) and Malvaceae (F). However, similarity in both size and shape need not imply a botanical relationship: A and B belong to different families.

Among the countries noted for their scientific work on pollens in honey are Switzerland, Germany, Denmark, Poland and France. Evidence from pollen analysis has led to many successful prosecutions for the sale of imported honey (which showed mostly exotic pollen grains) as home-produced honey, and at the higher price the latter commanded.

One survey has been made in Britain, on 726 samples from England, 94 from Scotland and 15 from Wales; also 20 from Ireland. In reporting on the results, A. S. C. Deans concludes that they:

provide interesting confirmation of the commonly held view that there are very few major honey sources which are of economic importance over most of the British Isles. Individual pollen analyses showed that white clover and heather were the only 'single-source' samples obtained. However, it was exceptional to find even these honeys with no contribution from other plants, and it is true in general that a great many different species contribute to any single jar of honey. This composite character of British honey is not detrimental, except in so far as it makes the production of a 'standard' honey difficult. It gives to our honeys a richness of flavour and aroma which is absent in honeys produced in countries where this multitude of 'minor' nectar sources is absent.

In certain localities, or in a season of abnormal weather, bees may produce honey from flowers not normally present in sufficient numbers to provide a flow. A knowledgeable observer can obtain and identify some unusual honeys; one such person is Dr. Annemarie Fossel at Ennstal in the Styrian Alps. She has found that pollen from rough gentian, *Gentiana aspera*, is a characteristic component (1–6 per cent) of honeys from some of the high meadows of the Salzkammergut. In 1956, 67 per cent of the pollen grains in one of her honeys were from great masterwort, *Astrantia major*, the first pioneer plant after some ground had been cleared; it was displaced after three years or so by nettles and raspberries. The *Astrantia* honey was bright yellow, thick, and with a sharp, almost bitter, flavour and aroma. Other local sources of Alpine honey, identifiable from their pollen grains, included the wax flower or lesser honeywort, *Cerinthe minor*, which is mentioned in Virgil's Fourth *Georgic*, box-leaved milkwort, *Polygala chamaebuxus*, and one of the bistorts, *Polygonum amphibium*.

Moving from the high Alps to coastal salt marshes, sea lavender, *Limonium vulgare*, yields quite large honey surpluses on both sides of the English Channel: in a few remote localities in Kent, and on islands off the Dutch coast, for instance. There are many other such examples.

Honeydew honey contains no pollen grains, but its microscopic components are equally indicative of the plant source of the honey. The most important are algal cells, chiefly from bark algae on the living leaves and conifer needles, and spores of sooty moulds, *fumago*, chiefly of the group of *fungi imperfecti*. An expert can often use these to identify the plant on which bees collected the honeydew.

4. Honey in the home

GENERAL GUIDELINES

Honey may be used in almost all circumstances in place of ordinary sugar, which is sucrose. But unless someone in your family keeps bees, honey will cost more than sugar, so it is sensible to use it where it has some special advantage. For instance the flavour of honey can be appreciated most in uncooked dishes. The moisture-retaining property of honey improves the keeping qualities of baked goods such as cakes and breads, and honey can give a better crust texture. Then there are certain traditional sweets and confectionery, where honey alone can give the proper consistency. Lastly, in dressings for meat and fish during roasting, honey spread over the surface can penetrate into the flesh, as dry sugar would not do.

First, here are some tips on the use of honey in general.

1. Liquid honey can be made more runny by warming it, and stiffer by cooling it. These changes are temporary, and depend on the viscosity of the honey which is very sensitive to temperature.

2. Liquid honey can be made to granulate within a few days, by stirring in a little honey that is already finely granulated. The crystals of this added honey serve as nuclei for the formation of further crystals throughout the liquid honey, which is super-saturated with sugars.

3. Granulated honey that is too hard for table use should be left in a warm place (30°C, 86°F) until it is soft enough to spread. It is unlikely then to return to its original hardness.

4. Granulated honey can be made liquid by standing the jar in fairly hot water for an hour or so, or by using a microwave oven as for defrosting. The tiny crystals dissolve in the liquid; once the honey is completely liquefied it may or may not change back into granulated honey.

5. Honey that is too thick to pour may be difficult to measure, but if the spoon or cup to be used is lightly greased, or dipped in cooking oil or boiling water, the honey will leave it more readily. Use of a spatula or rubber scraper will ensure that the full measure is used.

6. Honey is sticky, but it mixes readily with cold or hot water, and stickiness on fingers, fabrics, furniture or floors can be wiped off with water at whatever temperature is convenient.

7. In the course of time, a jar of granulated honey may show 'frosting': patterns of crystals appear at the interface between the honey and the glass jar, somewhat similar to the patterns of ice crystals on window panes in frosty weather, before the days of central heating. Frosting spoils the look of the honey, though not other qualities; it cannot be seen if honey is packed in opaque plastic containers, which is one advantage of their use.

8. Do not buy honey that has a layer of liquid at the top of the jar and paler crystallized honey below. The reasons for this separation, and for the chance of spoilage by fermentation, are explained in Chapter 3. If your own honey separates in this way in the jars, you can return it to its liquid state by following the directions in 4 above.

9. If, when you open a jar of honey you have just purchased, it looks or smells as if it had started to ferment, return it to the shop. It is not good value; whatever else may be at fault, its water content is too high. If any of your own honey should start to ferment, you will find that it is still satisfactory for baking or sweetening stewed fruit. The deliberate fermentation of honey to make mead is dealt with later in this chapter.

10. The recipes selected for this chapter are either traditional ones that have some special interest, or examples of what is considered be to currently useful. Most have been tested independently in two or more home kitchens, by members and staff of the International Bee Research Association.

A number of honey cookery books and leaflets are available, and health cookery books use honey in many of their recipes. Wherever you live, you should be able to obtain further recipes from a beekeepers' association or honey marketing authority, or through your honey supplier. Some, but not necessarily all, will have been professionally tested, and not all are reliable as to quantities.

HONEY AT THE TABLE

About 800,000 tons of honey are harvested in the world each year, and most of the honey sold on the world market is used as table honey (say 100,000 tons), usually spread on bread or something similar. This large amount of honey is eaten in its natural state, uncooked and unmixed with another product. There are not many foods of which the same can be said.

Having honey to put on one's bread was an indication of good living long before butter and jam were used in this way. The nursery rhyme in which 'The Queen was in the parlour, Eating bread and honey' dates back at least to 1600. By the beginning of the present century, if not before, honey carried with it an element of nostalgia for the good country things of a pre-industrial age. The ending of Rupert Brooke's poem 'The Old Vicarage, Grantchester' (1912) is often quoted:

> Ah, God! to see the branches stir
> Across the moon at Grantchester!
>
> . . . . .
>
> . . . oh! yet
> Stands the Church clock at ten to three?
> And is there honey still for tea?

It is no wonder that English tea-time is a noted occasion, for there are so many things to spread honey on. Oatcakes and biscuits (crackers) are good, more especially if they are hot so that the aroma of the honey is released. So are toasted bread and teacakes, scones, baps, waffles, crumpets and pancakes.

Many beekeepers prefer honey to sugar for sweetening their tea or coffee, and hot milk with a spoonful of honey stirred in is a favourite nightcap or pick-me-up. Liquid honey is delicious on fresh raspberries or blackberries, or grapefruit or melon, and by diluting the honey with a little hot water, it is easily poured from a jug.

Honey pots for household use can be collectors' items, especially those from the last century or earlier. There are various interesting private collections, and the IBRA has many examples of honey pots from different countries, both ornamental and utility; four of them are shown on the cover of this book.

15. Two metal screw-caps for honey jars, *c.* 1900.

In England, honey containers for use at the table date back at least to 1750. Some of the earliest were honey tureens for the combs of honey cut out of hives before any other method of harvesting honey had been devised. But the best-known type is a covered pot in the authentic or stylized shape of a straw skep; there is sometimes a separate stand, or one which is attached as with the silver pot shown on the cover of this book. Paul Storr made some elegant silver pots around 1800, one of which was sold for over £900 in London in the 1960s. Skep-shaped pots have been made in many ceramic materials, from earthenware to Wedgwood china and Worcester porcelain, and in pressed and slag glass. Some examples were and are beautiful, but some rather crude parodies of the traditional style can also be found, decorated with grotesque and misshapen bees. French and German honey pots reflects the local shapes of the skep, and there are attractive Italian and French honey pots like miniature apothecary's jars, with bee ornamentation; the one shown on the cover is inscribed *Miel roséat.*

Every household should try to have one elegant honey pot. Such objects are worth hunting for, and are eagerly sought by both amateur and professional collectors. Especially in tourist areas, true honey pots and other attractive pots are sometimes sold filled with honey inside a sealed plastic bag; warming may be necessary to extract the bag of honey through the opening.

Utility honey containers range from handmade earthenware pots, of which one is shown on the cover, to factory-produced glass and plastic jars. One primitive honey pot in the IBRA Collection, from the Arabian peninsula, is a small dried gourd with a triangular hole cut in it, through which the original contents were removed and the honey then inserted; the 'lid' was replaced over the hole and sealed, and the honey thus taken to market. The ornamented gourd honey container shown on the cover is from Mali in Africa.

Glass has been the most common material for utility honey jars since the 1860s, when a method was devised for separating the liquid honey from the wax comb. The jars have a wide mouth and, usually, a screw-top lid which in the early days might be stamped with some sort of a bee ornament, to designate the contents as pure and unadulterated bee honey. In many countries honey is now sold in standard squat glass jars holding 500 g or 1 lb, the jars being much lighter in weight than in earlier days. They are inelegant – tall narrower jars show off clear liquid honey to better advantage – but the honey can be served from a short jar, right to the end, with an ordinary jam spoon or teaspoon. Beekeepers' suppliers sell special honey spoons which have a projection on the stem for hooking over the rim of the jar. Most pots in which honey is purchased can be used for serving it at the table, and the honey's origin is usually clear for all to see from the label. The label, in fact, takes over from the ornamental pot. One rather elegant example is shown in fig. 16. Honey labels are much less expensive to collect than honey pots, and a collection is likely to comprise many hundreds of them.

Plastic containers are now taking the place of glass jars, in some countries more than others. In the USA there are tall plastic honey pots shaped like a stylized bear,with a nozzle at the top of the screw-on lid through which the honey is squeezed. This is possible only if the honey is liquid (not granulated), and if the temperature is high enough for the honey to flow freely. A more elegant, and very effective, pouring container is shaped like a glass jar with a tight lid incorporating a metal cut-off device that eliminates drips.

The important characteristics of a honey pot for the table are a tightly fitting lid, not too great a depth, and not too great a capacity; 500 g or 1 lb is enough.

16. Modern honey label using a skep-within-a-skep design that incorporates an old engraving. The producer's name and address would be printed below.

HONEY IN PREPARED FOODS

To enable readers to use recipes that they come across from other countries it is necessary to provide some information about weights and measures; these are almost unbelievably irregular, and nowhere have I been able to find the following information collected together.

In many countries the metric system is used; in cookery recipes, amounts are then normally measured by weight (grams), except that liquids are measured by volume (litres, millilitres). In Britain and some associated countries where ingredients are also measured by weight, pounds (lb) and ounces (oz) are still used; 16 oz = 1 lb (about 450 grams). Liquids are measured in pints, and one British pint of water weighs 20 ounces (0·57 litre). In the USA *all* ingredients are usually measured by volume, the unit being a standard cup*, half a US pint. A US pint of water weighs 16 ounces, so one cup of water weighs 8 oz (225 ml). A cup of sifted flour weighs only 4 oz, and a cup of fresh breadcrumbs even less. I find that a cup of granulated sugar now (1980) weighs 8 oz, but in past decades the crystals were less fine, and in 1937 one cup was reckoned as 5 oz.

Honey is one of the heaviest (highest density) foods, and a US cup* contains nearly 12 oz, a level tablespoon $\frac{3}{4}$ oz. Small amounts are measured everywhere by (level) spoonfuls, which are, however, variously defined; the UK, USA, Canada, and Australia all have different systems. Here:

> 1 tbsp = 1 standard (level) tablespoon = 15 ml = $\frac{1}{2}$ oz water
> 1 tsp = 1 standard (level) teaspoon = 5 ml = $\frac{1}{6}$ oz water.

The above paragraphs are enough to show why cooks sometimes get unsatisfactory results when they follow recipes from another country, or even dating from another decade; a unit described by a familiar word may represent an unexpectedly different amount.

Many housekeeping books nowadays give tables of conversions between pounds/ounces and grams, but it is not at all easy to obtain translations between oven temperatures and gas marks (for which there is no international standard), so some information is included here.

Description	°Celsius or °Centigrade	°Fahrenheit	Gas mark, UK
very cool / very slow	110	225	$\frac{1}{4}$
	120	250	$\frac{1}{2}$
cool / slow	140	275	1
	150	300	2
moderate / moderately slow / warm	160	325	3
	180	350	4
moderately hot / fairly hot	190	375	5
	200	400	6
hot	220	425	7
	230	450	8
very hot	240	475	9

When replacing sugar by honey in your own recipes, remember that honey contains 80 per cent sugar and 20 per cent water, but that honey is sweeter than sugar. For baking, use 25 per cent

---

* There are other 'standard' cups (e.g. British, 10 oz water), but in this book 'cup' means a US cup.

more honey than sugar by weight (100 g instead of 80 g, 5 oz instead of 4 oz), and reduce added liquid accordingly. By volume, one cup of finely granulated sugar as now sold in England or the USA weighs 8 oz; and this weight of sugar is contained in 10 oz honey (0·83 or ⅚ of a cup). Again, add rather less liquid. Until you have some experience, replace only half the sugar by honey; you will learn as you go.

Be suspicious of a recipe using the word amount (or quantity) without specifying volume or weight; one cup of honey has the same volume as one cup of sugar, but it weighs one and a half times as much.

In the recipes which follow, quantities are given according to all three systems, metric, British, and current American. But with these recipes and any others you use, it is necessary to work wholly in one system – the conversions are not exact.

USING HONEY IN UNCOOKED DISHES

Instant lemon refresher

	metric	British	USA
lemon	one	one	one
honey	50 g	2 oz	3 tbsp
ice cubes	six	six	six
water	800 ml	1½ pt	4 cups

Cut the whole lemon roughly into pieces. Put it in an electric blender and switch to maximum speed for a few seconds. Switch off. Add the ice cubes and water, and switch to maximum speed for ½ minute, then strain. Return to the blender, add the honey, and mix in.

Müsli

Müsli, in England called muesli or Swiss porridge, is eaten for breakfast, and enjoyed by a much wider circle of people than those who like health foods. Here is one recipe, to serve 4 or 5.

	metric	British	USA
orange	one	one	one
lemon, juice of	one	one	one
eating apples	two	two	two

	metric	British	USA
banana	one	one	one
raisins	25 g	1 oz	$\frac{1}{3}$ cup
chopped nuts	50 g	2 oz	$\frac{2}{3}$ cup
rolled (breakfast) oats	75 g	3 oz	1 cup
liquid honey	2 tbsp	2 tbsp	2 tbsp
milk or single cream	150 ml	$\frac{1}{4}$ pt	$\frac{5}{8}$ cup

Discard the peel and pith of the orange; separate the segments and chop them roughly into a bowl. Add the lemon juice. Peel and core the apples and grate them coarsely; add them, also the chopped banana and other ingredients. Serve immediately.

Any mixture of raw fruits can be used, but one ingredient at least should be sharp-tasting. Müsli made with fresh blackberries always reminds me of breakfasts eaten out of doors in golden September sunshine.

Honey and cream cheese icing for cakes

	metric	British	USA
honey, softened granulated	100 g	4 oz	$\frac{1}{3}$ cup
cream cheese	100 g	4 oz	$\frac{1}{2}$ cup
lemon juice	.......to taste.......		

Blend until smooth; be sparing with the lemon juice, to prevent the mixture becoming too liquid. Spread on any type of cake: if you like, sprinkle chopped or shredded nuts over the icing.

Honey-butter hard sauce

	metric	British	USA
butter	100 g	4 oz	$\frac{1}{2}$ cup
honey	100 g	4 oz	$\frac{1}{3}$ cup
lemon juice	1 tsp	1 tsp	1 tsp
....or more to taste....			

Cream the butter, and gradually beat in the honey. Add the lemon juice slowly and blend until smooth. To serve with the Christmas pudding, add brandy instead of lemon juice – very slowly. Use more than a teaspoonful, but not so much that it will not blend in.

Blackberry honey ice

	metric	British	USA
wild blackberries (can be seedy ones)	450 g	1 lb	4 cups
apple	175 g	6 oz	two
liquid honey	350 g	12 oz	1 cup
lemon juice	2 tbsp	2 tbsp	2 tbsp
water	200–250 ml	$\frac{1}{3}$–$\frac{1}{2}$ pt	1 cup
egg whites	two	two	two

Put the blackberries into a saucepan with the water, then the cut-up apples, which need not be peeled; the less water you can use the thicker the product will be. Cook gently, covered, until soft and pulped; when cool, press the mixture through a sieve. Stir in the honey and lemon juice. Put in the freezer until partly frozen, then fold in the stiffly beaten egg whites. Pack into freezer boxes and complete the freezing. To use, remove from the freezer say $\frac{1}{2}$ hour before serving, with ice cream wafers and/or cream if you wish. This amount serves eight people.

Honey-citrus dressing
This is simple, and the flavour interestingly different from what might be expected from the two ingredients: liquid honey and juice of orange, lemon or any other citrus fruit. For use on ice cream or other desserts try equal volumes (say 2 tbsp of each). For fish or savoury dishes try 1 tbsp honey to 3 tbsp lemon juice. You will discover whether you need to add more honey or more juice to suit your own taste.

Honey mint sauce
Use a pot (say 50 ml, 2 oz, $\frac{1}{4}$ cup) with a tight-fitting lid. Half fill with honey and warm it so that the honey is quite liquid. Stir in as much chopped fresh mint as it will take. This keeps well. If you store whole mint leaves in small plastic bags in the freezer, chopping is unnecessary. Crumble the leaves inside the bag, by crushing the bag from outside, while still hard frozen.

Light mayonnaise with honey

	metric	British	USA
egg	one	one	one
honey	1 tsp	1 tsp	1 tsp
lemon juice	2 tbsp	2 tbsp	2 tbsp
salt	½ tsp	½ tsp	½ tsp
dry mustard or French mustard	2 tsp	2 tsp	2 tsp
salad oil	150 g	¼ pt	⅝ cup

.... or as required ....

Put in the blender all ingredients except the oil. Cover, and mix at low speed. Leave switched on, and add the oil slowly through the central hole until the mixture is as thick as you like it. Adjust the flavour as required. This is a basic recipe, capable of many variations, by adding e.g. tomato purée, grated horseradish, or tart apples.

HONEY IN PRESENT-DAY BAKING

In general, when using honey for baking, combine it with other liquids before adding them to the dry ingredients. Bake at a fairly low temperature, both to prevent rapid browning and to reduce loss of honey flavour.

Spice gingerbread with honey

	metric	British	USA
plain flour	350 g	12 oz	3 cups
honey	175 g	6 oz	½ cup
brown sugar	75 g	3 oz	½ cup
melted butter	125 g	4 oz	½ cup
melted lard	125 g	4 oz	½ cup
eggs	two	two	two
milk (can be sour)	150 ml	¼ pt	⅝ cup
ground ginger	2 tsp	2 tsp	2 tsp
ground cinnamon	1½ tsp	1½ tsp	1½ tsp
ground cloves	½ tsp	½ tsp	½ tsp
salt	½ tsp	½ tsp	½ tsp
bicarbonate of soda	1 + tsp	1 + tsp	1 + tsp
sultanas and/or candied peel up to	125 g	4 oz	¾ cup

In a mixer (slow speed), or by hand, beat the eggs; add milk, sugar and spices, and beat well. Add to the mixture the melted butter and lard to which the honey has been added, then the flour with salt, ginger, soda sifted in, and lastly fruit and peel. Include some crystallized ginger if you have it. Beat very briefly. Pour into two flat tins about 25 × 20 cm (10 × 8 in), lined with greaseproof paper. Bake in a moderate oven (180°C, 350°F, gas 4) for 40 minutes. Cut into squares or fingers while hot. For storing or freezing, leave the gingerbread on the greaseproof paper.

This has been a standby in my family for over thirty years, but very much older recipes are given later.

Fresh lemon cake

	metric	British	USA
butter or margarine	125 g	4 oz	$\frac{1}{2}$ cup
mild-flavoured honey	175 g	6 oz	$\frac{1}{2}$ cup
eggs	two	two	two
milk	50 ml	2 oz	$\frac{1}{4}$ cup
flour	225 g	8 oz	2 cups
lemon juice	2 tbsp	2 tbsp	2 tbsp
grated lemon rind	$1\frac{1}{2}$ tsp	$1\frac{1}{2}$ tsp	$1\frac{1}{2}$ tsp
salt	$\frac{1}{2}$ tsp	$\frac{1}{2}$ tsp	$\frac{1}{2}$ tsp
bicarbonate of soda	$\frac{3}{4}$ tsp	$\frac{3}{4}$ tsp	$\frac{3}{4}$ tsp

Preheat the oven to 180°C (350°F, gas 4). In the large bowl of an electric mixer, or by hand, cream the butter and continue creaming while adding the honey in a fine stream. Add the eggs, one at a time, beating well after each. Sift together dry ingredients and add the lemon peel. Add these to creamed mixture alternately with the milk, beginning and ending with dry ingredients. Beat after each addition. Fold in the lemon juice. Pour into two greased 20 cm (8 inch) round sandwich tins. Bake for 20–25 minutes, until done in the centre. When cool, fill and ice as desired. I use lemon curd for the filling, and for the icing 75 g (3 oz, $\frac{2}{3}$ cup) icing sugar, 50 g (2 oz, $\frac{1}{4}$ cup) butter, and lemon juice – enough to flavour the icing but not enough to make it too soft.

Honey Anzac cookies

	metric	British	USA
margarine	125 g	4 oz	½ cup
honey	2 tbsp	2 tbsp	2 tbsp
flour	150 g	5 oz	1¼ cup
rolled (breakfast) oats	125 g	4 oz	1¼ cup
desiccated coconut	100 g	3½ oz	1¼ cup
soft brown sugar	175 g	6 oz	1¼ cup
bicarbonate of soda	1 tsp	1 tsp	1 tsp
hot water	1 tbsp	1 tbsp	1 tbsp

Melt margarine and honey. Meanwhile mix together flour, coconut, sugar and oats; dissolve soda in water. Mix everything together. Roll into small balls and put on a greased baking sheet; allow for spreading. Cook in a moderate oven (180°C, 350°F, gas 4) for 10–15 minutes until golden brown, or darker if you like them crunchy.

Bread made with honey

Extended studies on the usefulness of honey in baking have been made at Kansas State University, and the information here is adapted from Kansas *Bulletins* C-281 and 441. Very little sugar is needed in bread making, but if honey is used instead of cane sugar the bread keeps better, remaining moist, and its flavour is improved.

Recipes are given for white and wholemeal bread; alternatively you can use your own bread recipe and substitute an equal weight of honey for the sugar.

Two white loaves	metric	British	USA	Two wholemeal loaves
flour	700 g	1½ lb	5 cups	flour
milk	450 ml	⅘ pt	2 cups	milk
honey	2 tsp	2 tsp	2 tsp	honey
yeast	20 g fresh	¾ oz fresh	one cake compressed	yeast
shortening	25 g	1 oz	2 tbsp	–
–	20 g	¾ oz	1½ tbsp	shortening
salt	2 tsp	2 tsp	2 tsp	salt

Cream the yeast and honey. Warm the milk to 27°C (81°F); if

unpasteurized scald it first; add it to the yeast and honey and leave for 10 minutes. Work the shortening into the flour and salt, and add the liquid to make a smooth elastic dough. More liquid is needed with some flours than with others. Knead the dough well, and place it in a lightly greased deep container, warmed to 35°C (95°F), and cover tightly.

Set in a warm place (29°C, 84°F) for about 2½ hours or until the dough has doubled in bulk. Divide the dough into halves and knead lightly; let them rest for 10 minutes. Make into loaves and place each in a ½-kg (1-lb) baking tin. Cover the loaves with plastic or a damp cloth, which should not touch them.

White: return to the warm place for 50–60 minutes or until the loaves have doubled their size again.

Wholemeal: Brush the top of the loaves with warm water, to prevent crusting, leave to rise for 50 minutes or until the dough is 1–2 cm (½ in) above the tins.

Bake in a hot oven (220°C, 425°F, gas 7) until golden brown; the white bread will take about 40 minutes and the wholemeal about 50.

Windfall baked apples

In my own family this was one of the favourite desserts at apple time before freezers became commonplace, and it is still very popular. The amounts I use are roughly as follows:

	metric	*British*	*USA*
prepared apples	500 g	1 lb	5 large
sultanas	25 g	1 oz	⅙ cup
honey	25–50 g	1–2 oz	2–3 tbsp
butter or margarine	1 tbsp	½ oz	1 tbsp
water	8 tbsp	8 tbsp	8 tbsp

Peel and cut into quarters (or substantial slices) enough cooking apples to make a good layer in a shallow fire-proof dish. Sprinkle the sultanas on to them, then dollops of honey to sweeten, with a knob of butter or margarine on each. Cover the bottom of the dish with water, adding a little lemon juice if the apples are not tart. Bake in a moderate oven (160°C, 325°F, gas 3) until tender. Serve hot with cream.

HONEY FOR MEAT AND FISH

Honey-roast ham

One interesting present-day use of honey is in meat cookery. Boil or bake the ham (fat side up) according to whatever recipe you prefer, but 45 minutes before it will be done remove the rind from the ham and score it criss-cross, in diagonal lines. (If you baked the ham, pour off most of the fat from the tin.) Insert cloves into the flesh at the intersections of the criss-cross lines. Mix together the following dressing, and spread it over the ham; amounts are for about 1½ kg (3–4 lb).

honey	1–2 tbsp
orange juice	2 tbsp
grated orange peel	½ tsp

When the ham is glazed and brown, decorate it before serving with pineapple slices and, if you like, some glacé cherries. Instead of the orange juice and peel, you can use crushed pineapple, or cooked dried apricots, or a stiffish pulp of any rather tart fruit.

Honey-mint glaze for roast lamb

honey	1 tbsp
mixed orange and lemon juice	1 tbsp
chopped fresh mint*	1 tbsp

Mix the ingredients; stand them in a warm place while the joint of lamb is roasting (the top of the cooker is ideal). Then ½ hour before serving, drain off most of the fat and pour the glazing liquid over the joint. Return to the oven for the final ½ hour or so, and baste two or three times. Serve the sauce with the meat.

Trout with honey and almonds (per person)

	metric	British	USA
fresh trout	one	one	one
fresh thyme	sprig	sprig	sprig
lemon	slice	slice	slice
blanched almonds (chopped)	25 g	1 oz	3 tbsp
butter	25 g	1 oz	1½ tbsp

* See under Honey mint sauce, page 73.

honey	1 tbsp	1 tbsp	1 tbsp
dry white wine or dry sherry	1 tbsp	1 tbsp	1 tbsp
black pepper	.......to taste.......		

Clean as many trout as required, stuff with thyme and lemon slice, and lay in a buttered fireproof dish. Over them sprinkle the almonds, and black pepper, and scatter dabs of butter and honey. Pour the wine over all. Bake uncovered for 20–25 minutes at 220°C (425°F, gas 7). Garnish with more slices of lemon. Serve with fresh peas and buttered new potatoes.

MODERN VERSIONS OF THREE ROMAN SAUCES

The sauces below give an idea of the flavour of some of the dishes eaten in Ancient Rome. The relative amounts of ingredients are unknown, as quantities were not normally quoted before the seventeenth century. I am indebted to Philippa Pullar's book *Consuming passions* (Hamish Hamilton, 1970) for some of the information used here.

For roast pork. Rub a boned or chined loin of pork on both sides with the mixture on the left below; baste it while roasting with the mixture on the right.

Rubbing	Basting*
ground pepper	Worcestershire sauce substituted
ground coriander	for *garum*
ground fennel seed	oil
ground almonds	honey

To serve with pigeons and small birds. The mixtures are:

Rubbing	Basting
pepper	honey
lovage	pounded dates
coriander	chopped onion
caraway seeds	egg yolk
mint	Worcestershire sauce (for *garum*)
	very sweet wine, or grape juice
	oil

* Compare this with a 1975 English basting mixture for roast duck:
  2 good tbsp of honey
  1 tbsp wine vinegar
  ½ tbsp soy sauce
  1 teacupful (say ¾ cup) boiling water

To serve with fish. The mixtures are:

Rubbing	Basting
lovage	pounded hard-boiled egg yolks
cummin	pounded dates
marjoram (origan)	honey
mustard	chopped onion
	vinegar
	Worcestershire sauce
	oil

TRADITIONAL HONEY CAKES

The cakes, biscuits and cookies discussed below are direct descendants of very early baked foods, and are of interest on this account. 'Wafers made with honey' were familiar to the ancient Israelites, since this is how they described the manna they found in the desert after their flight from Egypt (Exodus 16:3). In one translation of the still earlier story of Abraham's hospitality to three auspicious visitors, 'Abraham hastened into the tent unto Sarah, and said, make ready quickly three measures of fine meal and honey, knead it, and make cakes upon the hearth' (Genesis 18:6).

Such cakes have been made for centuries throughout much of the Ancient World, and their very simplicity accords with the practices of nomadic peoples. They were introduced to Europe by returning Crusaders, if not by still earlier travellers. In subsequent periods a raising agent was incorporated, and also spices, and sometimes eggs. But these honey cakes (*pain d'épice*, *Lebkuchen**) contained no butter, and this in itself suggests an origin in a region where dairy products were not significant. In Czechoslovakia the flat cakes are now elaborately iced, and made up into complicated structures – e.g. gingerbread houses.

Many other areas had their own variants. Recipes for twenty-three honey cakes from regions of Belgium, northern and central France, Germany and Switzerland are included in a book by Pierre Paillon, *La fabrication des produits alimentaires*; only two of these recipes contain butter. A 1607 recipe for *pain d'épice de Reims* is worth quoting, because it gave quantities:

---

* French *pain d'épice* = 'spiced bread'; German *Kuchen* = cakes; the prefix *Leb*-may have come from the Latin *libum*, the sacrificial honey cake of Ancient Rome.

wheat flour	4 lb
boiled honey	1 lb
anise	2 oz
cinnamon, coarsely ground	2 oz
cloves, similarly	2–3 drachms (1 drachm = $\frac{1}{8}$ or $\frac{1}{16}$ oz)
cinnamon, similarly (*sic*)	2–3 drachms

Directions were as follows. Mix the ingredients into a paste with hot water, and a little rose water, and make into a flat cake. Sprinkle with ginger (and other spices), lightly ground.

Senlis was one town with a special reputation for its *pain d'épice*, and the street cry of those who sold it in Paris, 40 km to the south, was put on record around 1500:

Pain d'épice pour le cueur!	Honey spice cake for the heart!
Dans Senlis je le vois quérir,	In Senlis it is sought,
Qui d'avoir en aura désir	Anyone who wants a piece –
Je luy en donneray de bon cueur!	From me it can be bought!

Couques de Dinant

These Belgian cakes have been a speciality of Dinant since medieval times. Juliette Elkon in *The honey cookbook* remarks that they are 'the closest thing to the Biblical cake of flour and honey', and universal in Europe and the Mediterranean lands, wherever honey and cereals are to be found.

Put warm honey into a bowl and work in as much plain flour as you can, to make a stiff paste. The flour may be the same weight as the honey (three times the volume, i.e. three times as many cups), or somewhat less. Roll out to 1 cm thickness between sheets of waxed paper, and leave covered at room temperature, for two days if possible. Cut into circles or squares, or use a gingerbread mould – such as you can still buy in Dinant – to make a design in bas-relief on the upper surface. Bake in a slow oven (150°C, 300°F, gas 2) for 25 minutes. The cakes will keep indefinitely, and actually improve after a few months' storage. But they are by their nature hard, and the following recipes incorporate other ingredients that make a product more in keeping with present-day tastes.

Danish honey cake

This 'gingerbread' has become associated with Hans Andersen's fairy tales, but it must be based on the very early cake just discussed. It is a very good cut-and-come-again cake, and the spices provide additional flavour.

	metric	British	USA
honey	350 g	12 oz	1 cup
sugar	175 g	6 oz	$\frac{3}{4}$ cup
water	100 ml	$\frac{1}{5}$ pt	$\frac{1}{2}$ cup
eggs	two	two	two
plain flour	600 g	1$\frac{1}{4}$ lb	4 cups
ground cinnamon	1 tsp	1 tsp	1 tsp
ground ginger	1 tsp	1 tsp	1 tsp
ground cloves	1 tsp	1 tsp	1 tsp
orange peel, finely chopped	.... a little		
bicarbonate of soda	1$\frac{1}{2}$ tsp	1$\frac{1}{2}$ tsp	1$\frac{1}{2}$ tsp

Warm the honey, sugar and water gently (e.g. in a double boiler); do not let it boil. When cool, stir in the soda dissolved in a little water, and the beaten eggs. Add the spices and orange peel, then the flour, and mix thoroughly, but do not overbeat. Pour the batter into two greased and floured cake tins 20 cm (8 in) in diameter or in two $\frac{1}{2}$ kg (1 lb) bread tins. Bake in a slow oven (150°C, 300°F, gas 2) for 1 hour.

Serve sliced and buttered, or cut into two layers with butter filling between them.

Basler Leckerli

Kirsch enlivens these Swiss cakes; in some other countries brandy is used. Spices are a common ingredient, and also nuts and candied peel.

		metric	British	USA
honey		450 g	1 lb	1$\frac{1}{3}$ cups
kirsch		75 ml	6 tbsp	$\frac{3}{8}$ cup
sugar		225 g	8 oz	1 cup
flour	(about)	700 g	1$\frac{1}{2}$ lb	4–5 cups
shelled almonds, coarsely ground		150 g	5 oz	1 cup

candied orange and lemon peel, finely chopped	75 g	3 oz	½ cup
ground cinnamon	1 tsp	1 tsp	1 tsp
ground cloves	1 tsp	1 tsp	1 tsp
confectioner's glaze			

Bring the honey to the boil in a large saucepan, remove from the heat, and stir in the kirsch and sugar. Keeping the pan on medium heat, stir in the remaining ingredients except the flour and glaze. Remove from the heat again and gradually stir in the flour until the dough comes cleanly away from the side of the pan. If necessary add a little extra flour.

Roll out the dough on a floured board 1–2 cm (½ in) thick, and cut into pieces say 5 × 8 cm (2 × 3 in). Place them close together on a well greased and floured baking sheet. Leave them overnight at room temperature, then bake for 20–25 minutes in a moderate oven (180°C, 350°F, gas 4).

Brush with confectioner's glaze while still hot. Leave in an airtight container for 3–4 weeks to mature.

Swiss Lebkuchen

This recipe is enriched with cream as well as kirsch.

	metric	*British*	*USA*
honey	350 g	12 oz	1 cup
coffee	125 ml	⅕ pt	½ cup
double cream	200 ml	⅓ pt	1 cup
sugar	150 g	5 oz	⅔ cup
flour	600 g	1¼ lb	5 cups
kirsch	2 tbsp	2 tbsp	2 tbsp
ground aniseed	1 tsp	1 tsp	1 tsp
ground nutmeg	1 tsp	1 tsp	1 tsp
ground cinnamon	2 tsp	2 tsp	2 tsp
baking powder	1½ tsp	1½ tsp	1½ tsp
bicarbonate of soda	1 tsp	1 tsp	1 tsp

Blend honey, coffee, cream, sugar, kirsch and spices, then add the flour into which the baking powder and soda have been sifted. Beat until smooth. Turn into a well buttered baking pan and spread evenly. Bake 30–40 minutes in a moderate oven (180°C, 350°F, gas 4).

Turkish baklava

Baklava is a rather distant relative of the honey cakes discussed, and sometimes also contains spice. It is still widely made in Greece, Egypt and Turkey, but is probably of early origin.

		metric	British	USA
1	**For the pastry:**			
	plain cake flour	575 g	1¼ lb	5 cups
	eggs	two	two	two
	water	at least 2 tbsp	2 tbsp	2 tbsp
	salt	½ tsp	½ tsp	½ tsp
2	**For the filling:**			
	ground almonds	150 g	5 oz	1 cup
	skinned pistachio nuts	150 g	5 oz	1 cup
3	**Pour over before baking:**			
	unsalted butter	225 g	8 oz	1 cup
4	**Pour over after baking:**			
	honey	350 g	12 oz	1 cup
	water	225 g	8 oz	1 cup

Juliette Elkon's version runs as follows.   1. Sift the flour and salt into a bowl. Into a well in the centre pour the eggs, slightly beaten, mixed with the water. Blend in, then knead into a smooth paste, adding more water if necessary. Beat the dough with a rolling pin until it blisters. Divide into 30–40 pieces and roll each as thin as paper, so that they end up the same size and shape as your shallow baking tin. Lay the sheets singly on boards sprinkled with cornflour, and let them dry out for an hour.   2. Place 3 or 4 pieces on top of each other in the baking tin and sprinkle with some nuts and ground almonds. Continue alternating four layers of pastry and one of nuts, until the tin is three-quarters full.   3. Melt the butter and pour it over all; bake in a hot oven (230°C, 450°F, gas 8) for 20 minutes.   4. Remove from the oven and, while still hot, pour over the honey syrup, made by boiling the honey and water together, and cooling. When the baklava is cool, cut into small squares.

If the very thin pastry (sometimes called *filo*) can be purchased, the process becomes much simpler, starting at stage 2. In Cairo,

Sumaya Rashad made baklava for me in this way; she used a moderate oven, and a longer baking time – until the whole was golden brown. Baklava will keep indefinitely in an airtight container.

TRADITIONAL HONEY SWEETMEATS

Some of the regional sweetmeats made with honey have also maintained their importance through centuries of changing customs and life patterns. Recipes are given here, both to put them on public record and to enable readers who enjoy stepping backwards through time to do so, by reconstituting dainties such as must have been sampled by crusaders, pilgrims, and other medieval travellers. All have good keeping qualities, and a very high calorie value. They would thus have been suitable as snacks for the road, although they seem to have been eaten more usually as seasonal treats. Recipes are given below for:

torrone	from Italy
turrón	from Spain
nougat	from France (especially Montélimar)
halvah	from Turkey and Greece
pasteli	from Greece

Italian torrone

	metric	British	USA
honey	350 g	12 oz	1 cup
sugar	225 g	8 oz	1 cup
egg whites	two	two	two
roasted almonds, peeled	450 g	16 oz	3 cups
lightly toasted shelled hazel nuts	225 g	8 oz	1½ cups
mixed candied fruit	1 tsp	1 tsp	1 tsp
grated lemon rind	½ tsp	½ tsp	½ tsp
water	30 ml	2 tbsp	2 tbsp

Heat the honey in a double boiler, stirring with a wooden spoon, for about an hour or until golden. Add the stiffly beaten egg whites gradually, stirring constantly, until the mixture is white and fluffy. Boil the sugar and water together in a saucepan, without stirring, until caramelized. Add this mixture gradually to the honey-egg mixture, stirring constantly. Cook it all a little longer, until a small amount dropped into cold water forms a ball. Then add the nuts, candied fruit and lemon rind and stir immediately, before hardening starts.

Meanwhile, line two or three tins 15 × 20 cm (6 × 8 in) and at least 5 cm (2 in) deep, with rice paper (edible wafers)*. Pour a 5-cm layer of the mixture over the wafer, cover with another wafer layer and leave to cool. Finally cut the contents of each tin once lengthways. You will have 4–6 long pieces of *torrone*, which should be wrapped in waxed paper and kept in an airtight tin.

This recipe comes from Hedy Giusti-Lanham, an authority on Italian cooking and Executive Director of the American-Italy Society in New York.

Spanish turrón

This is traditionally made from rosemary or orange honey. Some 8,000 tons are manufactured for Christmas each year, mostly in Spain itself, where legislation governs standards for export.

	metric	British	USA
honey	250 g	9 oz	¾ cup
toasted almonds	350 g	12 oz	2½ cups
flour or fecula	.... as required		

Heat the honey until it boils, mix in the almonds, heat for a few minutes, then remove from the heat and sprinkle in a little flour or fecula. Spread the mixture over rice paper*, roll it flat with a rolling pin previously wetted, and cover with another layer of rice paper. Press under a weight for 10 minutes or so, then cut into whatever shapes you wish.

French nougat

	metric	British	USA
honey	350 g	12 oz	1 cup
sugar	450 g	16 oz	2 cups
light corn syrup or similar	6 tbsp	6 tbsp	6 tbsp
egg whites	three	three	three
blanched almonds, coarsely chopped	125 g	4 oz	1 cup

* If you cannot find rice paper in food shops, try a stationer's.

glacé cherries	75 g	3 oz	½ cup
water	225 ml	8 oz	1 cup
almond extract	1 tsp	1 tsp	1 tsp

Cook the honey, sugar, syrup and water to 130°C (265°F) on a confectionery thermometer. Add this syrup to the beaten egg whites, slowly, while still beating. When the mixture begins to stiffen add the other ingredients. Pour on to a buttered baking sheet lined with rice paper. Cover with waxed paper and press down with a weighted metal or plastic tray. Next day cut into strips and wrap in waxed paper. This is adapted from Juliette Elkon's recipe.

Greek halvah

	metric	British	USA
honey	350 g	12 oz	1 cup
olive or sesame oil	225 ml	8 oz	1 cup
chopped or ground nuts	125 g	4 oz	¾ cup
sugar	675 g	24 oz	3 cups
farina (or use cornflour)	375 g	13 oz	3 cups
water	225 ml	8 oz	1 cup
ground cloves	½ tsp	½ tsp	½ tsp
ground cinnamon	½ tsp	½ tsp	½ tsp

Boil the oil until it is very hot. Pour the farina into it gradually and stir slowly until the farina browns (30–45 minutes). Meanwhile make a syrup of the sugar, honey and water and boil it for 30 minutes. Add the spices and nuts. Mix the two lots. Stir constantly over slow heat until the mass thickens. Cover the pan for 5 minutes and then pour on to an oiled baking sheet. When cool, cut into squares and sprinkle with icing sugar or cinnamon. This recipe is also adapted from Juliette Elkon's.

Halvah (halewa) is also well known in Egypt, being eaten especially on the day celebrating the birth of Muhammad the Prophet. In 1978 I purchased ten varieties in Tanta, a town in the Nile Delta, but this commercial halvah is now made with sugar, not honey.

Greek pasteli

In Greece there are still thirty firms manufacturing this sweetmeat, producing altogether 5 million *pastelia* a year – a total of 400 tons.

	metric	British	USA
honey	275 g	10 oz	¾ cup
roasted sesame seeds	225 g	8 oz	2 cups
castor sugar	50 g	2 oz	⅓ cup

Boil all together slowly in a saucepan for 15 minutes or so, until golden brown. Test by dropping a little into cold water; when this sets hard, pour the mixture into a shallow tin, and after cooling cut it into pieces like toffee. Sesame seeds can be bought in a health food shop.

HONEY IN ALCOHOLIC DRINKS

Until the last century honey was extracted from the combs by draining them through a cloth bag. Afterwards, the combs and adhering honey were soaked in water and used for mead-making. Common definitions, which are followed here, are that mead was produced from the fermentation of honey and water only; the addition of herbs gave *metheglin*. Honey added to grape juice before fermentation yielded *pyment*; with herbs as well, the product was *hippocras*. Honey with apple juice fermented to *cyser* (containing more alcohol than cider, as *pyment* contained more than wine). Honey was also added to other alcoholic drinks after fermentation, to improve their flavour, and it might then be little changed. But in mead and related drinks, the honey sugars are fermented by yeasts into alcohol, in part (sweet mead) or entirely (dry mead).

Specific instructions for making mead do not survive from early times, but in principle the method was as follows. Water was added to the honey combs after most of the honey had been strained out, until the liquid would 'float an egg with all but a piece the size of a shilling [or some other coin] immersed'; the egg served as a primitive hydrometer. The mixture was then strained, the wax put aside for other use, and the liquid boiled to sterilize it, and skimmed. It was put into a barrel, and when cool enough 'set working like ale'. A piece of toast or other carrier primed with fresh ale-yeast was placed on top of the liquid; kept in a warm place, it would 'work' strongly for several days, then quietly for a few weeks or months, depending on circumstances, and in most households it would be used soon afterwards. Where mead-making was a professional activity – in Poland for instance – the best mead would be kept for several years before use. Many herbs and spices were sometimes added; the herbs were boiled in the water before it was added to the honey, and the spices – and commonly lemon peel – were put into the mixture to be fermented.

This same mead can be made today, and with our improved understanding of the processes of fermentation we can produce something better than our early forebears made. General instructions for home-made wines should be followed in making mead, and similar equipment is needed. Individual mead-makers differ on many points, and it would not make sense to combine methods. Two are summarized here: that of Brother Adam at Buckfast Abbey, who uses an updated and precisely described traditional method; and one such as is used by home wine-makers, from Brian Dennis.

Brother Adam points out that flavour, bouquet and character of mead result from the characters of the honey and the yeast, whereas its body and alcohol content depend largely on the proportions of honey and water, as follows.

Mead	Honey : water*	Relative density of must	Sugar content of must
sparkling, dry	2	1·053	13·0%
	2½	1·064	15·6%
dry, still	as above, or:		
	3	1·075	18·1%
	3½	1·086	20·6%
medium sweet	4	1·096	22·8%
to	5	1·114	26·1%
rich dessert	6	1·128	29·7%

* Number of pounds of honey per British gallon, or hectograms (100 g) per litre, of water; a US gallon needs only 80 per cent as much.

The relative density (at 15°C, 59°F) is included so that the concentration can be determined with a hydrometer if cappings are used. Moreover the relative density is directly related to the *sugar* concentration, which is more significant than the honey concentration, in view of the variation in the sugar content of honeys.

In Brother Adam's experience it is much more difficult to make small quantities of mead than a cask-full, partly because the temperature cannot be kept as constant except by using special apparatus, and partly because the liquid-to-container interface has a larger area in proportion to the volume. He emphasizes that vessels should be of wood, or of glass, stainless steel, etc., and never of iron, brass or galvanized metal, nor of stone earthenware, which is too cold.

Brother Adam's mead

1. Use only clean, pure rain water or distilled water.
2. Use only mild-flavoured honeys from unbrooded combs; ling heather honey also makes good mead, but needs special treatment not included here.
3. Sterilize the honey – water solution (must) by boiling it for 1–2 minutes only, and the vessels to be used for fermentation by washing them with hot water only. A wine or sherry cask is preferred. Pour the must into the cask while boiling hot, leaving head-space at the top; close the bung hole with a tight wad of cotton wool.
4. Use one of the pure-culture grape wine yeasts, such as are available at home wine-making shops. Brother Adam uses Maury, but regards Madeira or Málaga as satisfactory. Add the yeast when the must has cooled to 27°C (81°F); the amount, if in a liquid medium, should be not less than 1 per cent of the total quantity treated.
5. Immediately after adding the yeast, replace the cotton wool, or – preferably – use a fermentation valve. Add no chemicals whatsoever, except perhaps to make a very dry wine.
6. The 'stormy fermentation' will start after 1½ days (or more) and will be superseded in a few days by the primary fermentation, lasting 6–8 weeks in a light wine or 3–4 months in a heavy one. Keep the temperature constant at 18°–21°C (64°–70°F)

throughout the fermentation, which is best done in summer.

7. Then, or as soon as the mead has cleared, decant it, siphoning the clear liquor into a clean cask which has been fumigated with a sulphur candle.

8. Keep the cask in a cellar for two years, during which the after-fermentation will take place. 'To obtain a mead of character, a beverage that will surpass the finest wines produced from the juice of the grape', mature the mead in sound oak casks for a full seven years before bottling it.

Brian Dennis's mead

Brian Dennis sees no difficulty in producing mead in small lots, using glass or plastic containers: a bottle holding 2 or 5 litres ($\frac{1}{2}$ or 1 gallon), or more. Sterilize the containers for an hour or so, using cold bisulphate solution or household bleach diluted with 10 times the amount of water, and rinse well; beware of hot liquids that could crack them. Use a glass bubbler fermentation valve from a home wine-making shop. Brian Dennis measures the weight of the honey and the total volume of the must (not the volume of water added), and gives relative densities at 20°C (68°F):

Mead	Honey : total must*
very dry	2
dry	3
	$3\frac{1}{2}$
sweet	4
very sweet	$4\frac{1}{2}$
	5

The method recommended is set out below, in successive stages:

1. Boil honey and water for 10 minutes to sterilize them, removing any scum that forms.

2. Make a 'starter', using a small quantity of (sterilized) must plus additives (see 3); inoculate it with a wine yeast culture,

---

* Number of pounds of honey per British gallon, or hectograms (100 g) per litre, of must; a US gallon needs only 80 per cent as much.

following directions provided with the yeast. Add the starter to the main bulk as soon as this has cooled to 27°C (81°F).

3. Add to the must, before the yeast, the following amounts of nutrients (in grams); alternatively buy pre-mixed nutrients and follow the instructions provided with them.

	per gallon		*per 10 litres*
	Br.	*US*	
tartaric acid	5·2	4·2	11·4
citric acid	3·6	2·9	7·9
ammonium sulphate	4·0	3·2	8·8
potassium phosphate	2·0	1·6	4·4
magnesium sulphate	0·5	0·4	1·1
common salt	2·0	1·6	4·4

4. Seal the vessel with a fermentation valve, and keep it between 18° and 27°C (65°–81°F), preferably between 21° and 24°C (70°–75°F), for 3 weeks or longer if possible.

5. Leave the mead in the same vessel for 6–12 months, with the valve in place; the temperature is not so critical at this stage.

6. Siphon the clear liquor into clean bottles, filling them to 3–4 cm below the (new) cork. If any sediment forms, cork for a week or two and then decant into fresh bottles.

Honey vinegar
Honey vinegar, which still has the aroma of honey, is made by fermentation of mead in the presence of air. Use 1 part of honey to 6 parts of water by weight, and the same proportion of nutrients as for mead. At the end of the alcoholic fermentation, or after about a month, add a culture of *Acetobacter aceti* or 'mother of vinegar'. At room temperature (15°–25°C, 60°–75°F) the mead should be converted into vinegar in 6–9 months. The acid fermentation can be speeded up to 1 month or less by circulating the mead over shavings carrying the *Acetobacter aceti*. Siphon off the vinegar and store in clean bottles.

Two other honey drinks
Two potent Scottish drinks should be mentioned: atholl brose and Drambuie. Atholl brose is not difficult to make. Following Meg Dod's recipe (1826), you start with a pound of dripped (best

quality liquid) honey, put into a basin with sufficient cold water to dissolve it (about a teacupful). Stir with a silver spoon. When well mixed, add gradually 1½ pints (0·85 litre) of whisky. Stir briskly until a froth begins to rise. Bottle and keep tightly corked.

Drambuie is said to be a contraction of *an dram buideach*, Gaelic for 'the drink that satisfies'. It is made from a 'secret recipe' incorporating honey and whisky, said to have come to Scotland with Bonnie Prince Charlie in 1745 and to have been given by him to a Captain MacKinnon in gratitude for refuge from his pursuers. The secret has been passed on from generation to generation, the last occasion being in 1973, on the death of Mrs. Georgina MacKinnon, then Chairman of the Drambuie Liqueur Company.

History of mead

One striking piece of evidence for man's early use of honey to produce alcohol is the fact that in virtually all Indo-European languages the same word-root *medhu-* is used to describe the product. In many languages this word-root is used even for alcoholic drinks in general. The present-day words include, for example, English *mead*, Dutch *mede*, Welsh *medd*, Czech *med*, *Russian mjod*, German *Met*, Scandinavian languages *mjöd*, Icelandic *mjöður*, Irish *miodh*, Hindi *madh*, Sanskrit *mádhu*.

Mead was probably a rarity in the civilizations of Ancient Greece and Rome, for although their literatures have many references to bees and honey, there are very few to a honey-based drink. Indeed the Greeks seem to have regarded it as alien, barbaric, and having its proper place in distant antiquity: 'Men at the first beginning used acorns for their bread and honey for their drink.' In Rome, Latin lost the root *medhu-* altogether, and at an early stage the Greek stem *meth-* came to denote alcohol generally (e.g. *méthusos* – drunk); the same stem is the basis of our *methylated spirit*.

Here are a few of the many mementoes of the importance of mead in and before medieval times. When Pytheas (334 BC), a contemporary of Alexander the Great, sailed to lands round the North Sea, he noted that people there ate honey and made a drink from fermented honey and grain. The banqueting hall at Tara, seat of the High Kings of Ireland up to AD 727, was *tech midchuarta*, house of mead-circling. There are various stories of angels refreshing themselves with mead.

An Anglo-Saxon riddle has survived, to which the answer was 'mead'; it would have been in vogue in England before AD 1000:

I am cherished by men, found far and wide, brought from the groves and from the city-heights, from the dales and from the downs. By day wings bore me in the air, carried me with skill under the shelter of the roof. Afterwards men bathed me in a tub. Now I am a binder and scourger; straightway I cast a young man to the earth, sometimes an old churl. Straightway he who grapples with me and struggles against my strength discovers that he must needs seek the earth with his back, if he foresakes not his folly ere that. Deprived of strength, doughty in speech, robbed of might, he has no rule over his mind, feet, nor hands. Ask what is my name, who thus on the earth in daylight binds youths, rash after blows.

In AD 1015 a fire in the German city of Meissen was extinguished with mead because of lack of water.

In 1460 there were thirteen establishments producing mead in Eger (Cheb) in Czechoslovakia, which was a well known mead-making town. Some large quantities of mead were produced in other countries too. In 1548 King Christian III of Denmark demanded 66 tons of it from his vassals, and 24 tons were consumed at the wedding of a princess in 1590.

There are records of several sovereigns of England drinking metheglin. For instance, Samuel Pepys entered in his diary for 25 July 1666: 'Dined with two or three of the King's servants, where we dined with the meat that came from his table; which was most excellent, with most brave drink cooled in ice, which at this hot time, was welcome; and I, drinking no wine, had metheglin for the King's own drinking, which did please me mightily.'

Wassail! in mazers of mead by Colonel G. R. Gayre (Phillimore, 1948) was published during a post-war revival of interest in honey-based drinks. It gives a well documented historical account of mead, metheglin, pyment, and hippocras, and in addition of mulsum, clare, and bracket. He also describes the horns, mazers, and mether cups out of which it was drunk. The book quotes the riddle cited above.

HONEY IN NUTRITION

A useful way to start considering the nutritional value of honey is to compare the amounts of various substances in it with the dietary requirements for these substances. Dietary requirements are commonly expressed in terms of the 'recommended daily intake', and Appendix 2 (Table 13) lists recommendations from both the UK and the USA. Honey contains many constituents that are valuable nutrients, but (apart from sugars) in very small amounts, even granted a generous daily ration of 100 g; the highest national average honey consumptions are no more than 2–5 g a day.

It is therefore unlikely that eating honey will correct deficiencies of trace elements or other substances in the diet. A similar table could be compiled giving the amounts of 18 amino acids in honey, but since the total weight of amino acids in 100 g honey is only a few mg, the weight of each one is of scientific interest rather than nutritional significance.

For infants, children, old people, and invalids, honey can be a more easily digested and more palatable carbohydrate food than, say, cane sugar, and there are many who believe that honey has a definite place in infant feeding. One detailed but rather little-known study was published by Sakari Lahdensuu in Finland in 1931. His 91-page report showed that honey was a satisfactory substitute for the sugar that constituted 5–7 per cent of the total daily food of twenty healthy infants. The best proportion of honey was 7–10 per cent. Weight gains were higher during the period when honey was added to the daily milk than when sugar was used, and the babies showed no tendency to diarrhoea. Measurements on the blood sugar and urine gave no indication that physiological processes were anything but normal when honey was used, nor was there any trouble with sugar or excessive acidity in the urine.

Many reports, based on clinical trials, conclude that honey can be beneficial to heart patients, and after strokes and operations. It has been suggested that the rapid assimilation of fructose may be associated with increased nitrogen retention, and also that the presence of invertase in honey is helpful for old and sick people. But if the benefits of honey are due to a unique mystical component, as some would claim, then this substance has not yet been identified, although 181 substances have been found in honey to date.

As a food, honey is a readily acceptable and easily digestible source of carbohydrates. Honey can be obtained in a form as near to a 'natural' food as almost any other, and this in itself is attractive to many consumers.

HONEY IN FIRST AID

In Ancient Egypt honey was the most popular medicament of all; it is mentioned some 500 times in the 900 remedies that are known. Honey was also a common ingredient of medieval medicines, for it was often the only substance available to make some of the more nauseating ingredients palatable. But in early cures and remedies, for instance those described in medieval leech books, honey seems to be cited even more frequently for external than for internal use. An early eleventh-century Anglo-Saxon manuscript in the Wellcome Historical Medical Library in London has one recipe that starts: 'To make yourself an ointment for tumours, one shall take pure honey such as it is used to lighten porridge ...'; a list is then given of juices of various herbs which may be incorporated. Among mentions of honey in the eleventh-century *Leechbook of Bald* are: as a component of 'the best eye salve'; for treating styes, 'foul' wounds, and internal wounds, and for use after amputations and to help the removal of scabs.

Many properties have been attributed to honey which have no foundation in fact – as a cure for serious disorders such as consumption and the plague. Nevertheless, honey is used today in hospitals in other specific circumstances, and is a component of various proprietary and dispensed medicines.

Honey as a dressing for wounds and burns

Honey has antibacterial effects, for instance on *Salmonella*, *Staphylococcus aureus*, *Micrococcus flavus*, *Bacillus cereus*; and it can be applied to wounds that are awkwardly placed for dressing.

In contact with any fluid, honey becomes diluted; the enzyme glucose oxidase in it then reacts with the glucose to produce gluconolactone and hydrogen peroxide. The hydrogen peroxide is unstable and decomposes, but its continuous generation gives the honey solution a bactericidal property. Years before this was understood, the property was attributed to an unknown substance in honey which was called 'inhibine' because it inhibited bacterial growth. The inhibine was destroyed if a solution of honey was exposed to light – a property characteristic of hydrogen peroxide.

There are many empirical reports that burns dressed immediately with honey heal well, without infection, and also with less scarring than after most treatments. But a casualty officer would probably say burns should receive no treatment at all until the patient reaches him.

The following is a story taken from a book of recipes compiled in the seventeenth and eighteenth centuries, but there is no way of checking its veracity. 'At Rome a Lady had the misfortune to be severely burned almost all over her whole Body by her Cloathes taking fire. To give temporary ease to the Torture a Domestic had recourse to some Honey, which had so good an effect that in Nine Days she was perfectly cured by use of this remedy alone.'

Honey has been used successfully in hospitals as a surgical dressing for open wounds, proving to be more comfortable than most dressings because – surprisingly – the dressing does not stick to the skin or the wound. Successful treatment with honey of amputations and badly infected wounds, bed sores, and skin and varicose ulcers, and especially ragged wounds difficult to dress, has been reported in hospitals in England and New Zealand. So honey can be regarded as a useful first aid treatment for wounds, and if by chance children or animals lick it off, it will not harm them.

After hospital surgery or minor injuries, it is not easy to apply dressings to a damaged area of mucous membrane. There have been recent reports of dramatic success after undiluted honey was poured into extensive and intransigent wounds made in operations for carcinoma of the vulva, and of the uterine body. The wounds became bacteriologically sterile within 3–6 days, and remained so. Honey is non-irritant, and promotes the rapid growth of healthy granulation tissue. Liberal application with undiluted honey has been found to bring complete relief of the tiresome symptoms of pruritus vulvae, after other treatments had failed.

When someone is 'out of sorts'
Many people find that honey added to their favourite nightcap, such as hot milk or whisky, makes a soothing mixture, and honey with hot lemon is favoured for colds. Honey can be very useful

for a sick child, and may also be successful in getting sick animals to start eating again; the main sugars in honey (glucose and fructose) are absorbed directly into the blood. Honey can also make unpalatable medicine acceptable, as it did in the Middle Ages.

One expensive 'elixir' on the market is advertised as being made from honey, yeast, herbs and orange juice. Honey and orange juice always make a good combination; you could try mixing in some ground-up yeast tablets and herbs, if you do not mind the change in flavour. It can do you no harm, and you might find it invigorating.

Coughs and colds

At least 200 tons of honey on the world market are purchased each year for use in commercial cough mixtures and sweets. Many people find that honey and lemon juice, taken a little at a time, helps them when they have a cough or ticklish throat. Try two tablespoons of honey to one of lemon juice; if you like it more bland, add a tablespoon of glycerine as well; menthol and eucalyptus oil are among the additives used in the trade. Or copy Samuel Pepys the diarist, who visited Mr. Bowyer one day in 1660 'despite a heavy cold ... Here I lay, and took a spoonful of honey and a nutmeg, scraped for my cold by Mr. Bowyer's direction.'

Hay fever

A number of hay fever sufferers report that their symptoms are alleviated if they eat the cell cappings that are sliced off honey combs before the honey is extracted from them. The effects may be produced partly by the chewing necessary before the cappings (beeswax with honey attached) can be swallowed. It is unlikely to work with everyone, but it is a simple, harmless thing to try if you are afflicted with hay fever.

Honey for hangovers

Honey contains 40 per cent of fructose, which is known to speed up oxidation of alcohol by the liver, and it is used for sobering up drunken patients. Honey has been found more effective than fructose, a fact that is attributed to the enzymes in honey, notably catalase. Some people eat honey *before* drinking alcohol, regarding it as a preventive measure. Hangovers are worst from drinks high in congeners – substances that give the drink its distinctive aroma and flavour – because these also produce toxic effects. Fructose and vitamin C are said to be helpful in eliminating the congeners from the body; so a treatment that has been recommended for a hangover is honey with lemon juice, say two tablespoons of honey and as much lemon juice as you like.

HONEY IN COSMETICS

A notice in *Fraser's Advertiser*, published in London in January 1835, ran as follows:

May's medicated honey for softening the skin, and preventing and curing chapped hands, lips, etc. When the face, hands, or lips, are rendered rough or chapped, whether by the use of hard water, or exposure to cold winds, one or two applications of the above will prove its decided superiority to any of the usual remedies, such as Cold Cream, Lip Salve, or Pomade Divine. It may be used on the most delicate infant; it imparts an agreeable perfume, and being applied while the parts are wet, the well known adhesive property of honey is entirely destroyed. Sold in Pots, 1s 1½d each, by the Proprietor, 4 Butter-market, Reading.

In 1972 Charles Revlon introduced his Skim Milk Natural/ Organic Skincare, incorporating two balms laced with 'nature's own moisturizer – pure, natural Clover Honey', with the declaration: 'I believe I have tapped a great new natural resource of beauty in 100% fat-free milk, rich with proteins … and moisturizing honey. Nothing I have seen gives skin such a look of vitality as these pure, natural organic ingredients.' Another advertisement in the same year read: 'Country fresh faces come to town with Mary Quant's new Special Recipes. A new and exciting range of cosmetics, packed full of natural ingredients including extracts of wheatgerm, honey, oil of almonds and beeswax.'

If you want to make honey cosmetics to use yourself, or to give for presents, here are recipes based on some from Russia, where the composition of cosmetics is not a trade secret. Their cost will be only a small fraction of that of the advertised products. Many have their origin in recipes used centuries ago, when honey was a wholesome ingredient of cosmetics among many that were not – preparations of lead and arsenic, for instance. There is plenty of evidence for the use of honey in cosmetics in Ancient Egypt.

Honey-water for cleansing the skin

	metric	British	USA
high quality honey	2 tbsp	2 tbsp	2 tbsp
warm water	1 litre	2 pints	2½ pints

Dissolve the honey in the water, then add 3 times as much warm water and wash the face and neck for 10 minutes. Rinse with warm water.

Honey face packs

For a single application, use one teaspoon of liquid honey, and mix in the following:

honey and glycerine	{	1 tsp glycerine
		1 egg yolk
honey and oatmeal	{	1 tbsp fine oatmeal
		1 egg yolk
honey and sour cream	{	1 tsp sour cream
		1 egg yolk

For a reserve supply, use 100 g (4 oz, ⅓ cup) of liquid honey, and mix in the following:

honey and alcohol face pack (standard)	{	25 g alcohol or surgical spirit (2 tbsp)
		25 g distilled or boiled water (2 tbsp)
honey and flour face pack (for dry skin)	{	60 g white flour (2 oz, ¼ cup)
		60 ml water (4 tbsp)

Cleanse the skin thoroughly, apply a hot compress for 2–3 minutes to open the pores and improve the circulation, then apply the face pack in a thin layer with cotton wool and leave for 15–20 minutes. Wash off with warm or tepid water.

Honey and cucumber lotion

	metric	British	USA
first quality honey	100 g	4 oz	⅓ cup
cucumber juice	100 g	4 oz	½ cup
40% alcohol	100 ml	¼ pint	½ cup

Add the juice from fresh cucumbers to the alcohol (Russians use vodka), and leave sealed in a cool dark place for 8 days. Then filter the infused liquor and mix with the honey.

Wash the face and neck with tepid water, and apply the lotion with a piece of muslin. Apply once a day, preferably an hour or so before going to bed.

English cosmetic cream

	metric	British	USA
white beeswax	50 g	2 oz	¼ cup
anhydrous lanolin	30 g	2 tbsp	2 tbsp
avocado oil	150 ml	¼ pt	½ cup
honey	15 g	2 tsp	2 tsp
scent	.......as required.......		

Melt the first three ingredients together in a double boiler, remove from the heat and stir until cool, but keep back a little of the oil to adjust the consistency at the end. Mix the honey in well, and finally the scent. Pot into small screw-top jars. This recipe is based on one in the December 1977 issue of *Good Housekeeping*, which illustrates a pot labelled Neck Cream. Lanolin can be obtained at a chemist, and avocado oil from health food shops.

English honey hand cream

	metric	British	USA
lard	100 g	4 oz	½ cup
egg yolks	2	2	2
honey	1 tbsp	1 tbsp	1 tbsp
ground almonds	1 tbsp	1 tbsp	1 tbsp
almond essence	.......a few drops.......		

This is an early Victorian recipe, said to work wonders for chapped hands. Soften the lard, mix it with the egg yolks and then the other ingredients to form a stiff paste.

Honey for the hair
Sarah, the beautiful Duchess of Marlborough, died in 1744 at the age of 84. Shortly before her death, Lady Mary Wortley Montagu wrote that she had 'the finest hair imaginable, the

colour of which she said she had preserved unchanged by the constant use of honey-water'. (*Letters*, ed. Wharncliffe, 1893)

Honey-water is made by mixing 2 tablespoons of honey with a litre of warm water.

5. Honey in the past and present

The history of honey is a long and fascinating one. Our knowledge of some of its earliest phases has been enriched by recent researches in anthropology and archaeology, and even in the development of languages.

Most early civilizations prized honey very highly, and both honey and bees were regarded as sacred. Bees were in fact making honey long before man existed, and almost certainly man enjoyed it from his very beginnings; he 'hunted' for honey as for many other foods. In many parts of the world honey hunting was superseded by beekeeping, a craft which remained almost unchanged for thousands of years, until there was an explosive development in the second half of the last century, which opened the way for the establishment of honey as a world commodity. Honey, the food that bees have produced for twenty million years, is now handled by machine and transported across the world.

HONEY BEFORE MAN

The following rough time scale shows the antiquity of bees and honey compared with that of man:

for 150–100 million years	flowering plants have existed and produced nectar and pollen
for 50–25 million years	solitary bees have existed, also early primates (monkeys)
for 20–10 million years	social bees have produced and stored honey
for a few million years	man has existed and has eaten honey
for ten thousand years	records have survived of man's exploitation of honey.

Honeybees, *Apis*, were among the social bees that evolved in the

Old World. Their colonies nested in hollow trees, in crevices in rocks, and in holes in the ground and, as they still do today, they collected and stored pollen, collected nectar, and made and stored honey. Honeybees could survive in any region where plants provided sufficient food to last the colonies through the next dearth period. There are four *Apis* species today; three are tropical: *Apis florea* and *Apis dorsata* which build a single comb in the open for a nest, and *Apis cerana* which nests in a cavity – as does the fourth species, *Apis mellifera*, which colonized the temperate zone in Europe and adjacent areas.

During the successive glaciations known as the Ice Age – which started something less than one million years ago and recurred at intervals until 10,000 years ago – *Apis mellifera*, with other animals in the northern regions, were driven southwards. Certain areas remained unfrozen, and these provided safe retreats for long periods until the climate improved again. Bee populations then spread out to adjoining areas by swarming, a daughter colony establishing itself in a cavity of an acceptable size, sheltered from the weather, and with an entrance small enough to be protected against robbers. The existence of suitable nesting places is a necessary condition for the natural spread of honeybees, and is sometimes the limiting one.

There were no indigenous honeybees in any part of the New World – the Americas and Australasia – but social 'stingless' bees and social wasps stored honey in some of the tropical areas there, and in the Old World tropical areas of Asia and Africa.

All these insects produced honeys that might well be hard to distinguish from the honeys produced by their descendants today, except in so far as the distribution of plants has changed. And however cleverly man exploits the bees, they are in principle no more 'domesticated' today than before man existed.

In a large part of the Old World, honeybees have thus been producing honey from flowering plants, and probably also from honeydew, for 10–20 million years. From the beginning, honey has been stored by bees and used by them later in the year; then, as now, the honey was sometimes taken instead by various mammals – although not yet by man – and also by other insects, and by birds. (Many other birds have names such as honeyeaters or honey-creepers, but these suck nectar from flowers, and a fifth

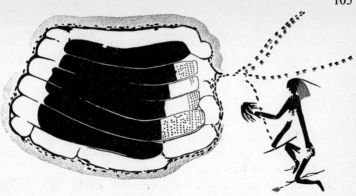

17. Rock paintings of a honey hunter near the Toghwana Dam, Matopo Hills, Rhodesia (the only rock painting known where the use of smoke is shown).
Scale 1 : 6.

of the world's birds are involved in flower pollination.)

We can get an idea of ways in which animals took honey or other food from bees' nests during the ten million years or more before man's appearance, by observation of similar animal marauders today. A bear – the best-known of the animals that like honey – receives many stings when extracting combs from a bees' nest, in spite of its protective coat. Bears are a nuisance to beekeepers in many parts of the world today, pulling hives apart and taking the boxes containing honey into the woods nearby, in an attempt to get rid of pursuing bees.

Primates also take honey. Baboons adopt quite elaborate measures to try to rid the honey comb of bees, and chimpanzees have been seen poking a long twig down the hole that led to the nest and withdrawing it coated with honey. Honey hunting by primitive man was thus a continuation of much earlier animal behaviour: robbing bees' nests, devising a way of getting the comb partially free from bees, and using a tool to extract the honey from the nest.

PRIMITIVE HONEY HUNTING

A number of Bushman paintings in rock shelters in Southern Africa portray honeybees and their combs, and some of them show ladders and other equipment used in honey hunting. One even shows a honey hunter using smoke to drive the bees away from their nest (fig. 17). Harald Pager, who has found and copied

18. Rock painting at Barranc Fondo, Castellón, Spain, showing honey collection from a bees' nest (with bees flying round), reached by a ladder. As well as the five figures on the ladder, a group lower down appear to be waiting to share the honey.
Scale 1 : 3·5.

many such paintings, has recently published drawings from part of the Altamira caves in northern Spain, and he argues persuasively that these drawings also represent combs and honey-hunting ladders, although they can be dated from 15,000 to 10,000 BC, towards the end of the Ice Age.

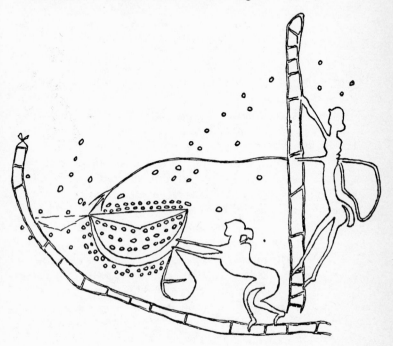

19. Rock painting *c.* 500 BC, showing honey being collected from the single large comb of an *Apis dorsata* nest, at Singanpur, India.

A rock painting at Bicorp in eastern Spain, reported in 1924, is somewhat later, perhaps 7,000 BC; but it also shows a honey hunter at the bees' nest, holding a bag to take the combs, and Dr. Lya Dams has recently reported several similar paintings in the same area (fig. 18). A lively rock painting in India (fig. 19) shows a tricky moment in gaining access to a nest of the largest species of honeybee, *Apis dorsata*. This bee is even today the source of a substantial part of India's annual honey harvest, which is collected by hunters in the age-old style. Heinrich Harrer describes the process in his *Seven Years in Tibet* (Hart-Davis, 1953):

This honey taking is a very risky adventure as the bees hide the honeycomb under projecting rocks of deep ravines. Long bamboo ladders are dropped, down which men climb sometimes two or three hundred feet, swinging free in the air. Below them flows the Kosi and if the rope which holds the ladder breaks it means certain death for them. They use smoke balls to keep the angry bees away as the men collect the honeycomb, which is hoisted up in containers by a second rope. For the success of this operation, perfect and well rehearsed combination is essential, as the sound of shouts or whistles is lost in the roar of the river below.

In the wild, honeybees commonly nest in hollow trees or rock crevices rather high above the ground. But this is not always so, and the Old Testament provides a clear description of early honey hunting where the harvest was more accessible. In I Samuel 14: 25–27: 'There was honeycomb in the country-side; but when his men came upon it, dripping with honey though it was, not one of them put his hand to his mouth for fear of the oath [Saul had forbidden eating until nightfall]. But Jonathan had not heard his father lay this solemn prohibition on the people, and he stretched out the stick that was in his hand, dipped the end of it in the honeycomb, put it to his mouth and was refreshed.'

In early times honey was thus a much prized food, which the hunter would often share with others of the group, as did Samson (Judges 14: 8–9): 'He turned aside to look at the carcass of the lion, and he saw a swarm of bees in it, and honey. He scraped the honey into his hands and went on, eating as he went. When he came to his father and mother, he gave them some, and they ate it.'

In general, what was eaten was not what is now called 'table honey'; it was the comb as it was broken off from the nest – wax, honey, pollen, bee brood, and probably a few dead bees as well. The pollen and brood would provide protein, which honey does not, and the whole would be both sweet and nutritious.

HONEY FROM HIVES

The earliest known record of keeping bees in hives and harvesting honey from them dates from 2400 BC, in Egypt (see fig. 20). The methods of getting honey from the bees changed very little during the next four thousand years. Indeed these methods were not so very different from those used in honey hunting, except that the

20. Drawing from a painted relief in the tomb of Rekh-mi-re (1450 BC) at Thebes, Upper Egypt, showing jars being filled with honey and sealed; on the right, combs are being taken from hives with the aid of a smoker. This relief is more explicit and better preserved than the fragmentary remains of a painting showing similar hives, which was in the sun temple erected by Ne-user-re at Sakkara, near Cairo, *c.* 2400 BC.

bees were in movable hives which the beekeeper could place where it suited him – close to his dwelling or somewhere else safe from predators. In many parts of the world the hives were in fact hung or fixed in trees and, like wild bees' nests, accessible only by using ropes or ladders.

There were gradual advances in managing bees in order to get more honey more efficiently and, from about AD 1600 onwards, experiments were made that led finally to the breakthrough that initiated the system of honey production now used.

The shift from hunting honey to keeping bees in man-made hives must have occurred independently in many places, and I think that in any area it followed one of several patterns. The concept of ownership of trees containing bees' nests was widespread. The rights of the owner were accepted and respected, although other men of his group would help him to get at the nest and open it up. Examples are known from tropical Asia and Africa, and there is full documentary evidence of extensive tree beekeeping in the forests of northern Europe during the Middle Ages. Dorothy Galton in *A thousand years of beekeeping in Russia* relates:

Bee walks [paths along which there were bee trees] were often mentioned in wills and deeds of the time, the lands often being left to monasteries. Whether trees had bees in them or not, they were not allowed to be felled, for bee-less holes could be used later by swarms. In a charter of 1565 the people of a village were forbidden to cut down bee trees with or without bees. There were frequent disputes about ownership of and rights in bee forests ... The Code of Ivan the Great (1550) laid down fines for destroying and robbing bee trees.

21. Woodcut published in 1774, showing honey harvesting from bee trees, similar to that carried out during and after the Middle Ages; see text for details.

Honey was as important, and was harvested in the same way, in western Europe. Fig. 21, an engraving from a German book published in 1774, shows two trees being worked for honey. The beekeeper on the left is in a sort of bosun's chair; the one on the right is up a ladder and seems to be wearing a protective mask. In each tree a rectangular door has been cut to provide easy access to the nest, and the bees were in fact 'worked' as in a hive, though the 'hive' would not be so called until it was cut from the tree. The

German word *Bienenstock*, meaning beehive, refers to a tree trunk.
Just to the left of the hands of the would-be helper standing on
the ground is the owner's mark on the tree, a cross; trees still exist
marked in this way. The centre figure (151) is a traditional *Zeidler*
[forest beekeeper] with his bow and arrow.

Records of this particular type of forest beekeeping abound in
continental Europe, but not in Britain. However, in November
1975 Frank Vernon took me into the New Forest in Hampshire
to see several trees he had just learned of, which showed clear
evidence that rectangular holes had been cut in them to provide
access to bees' nests, and doors fitted over the holes, which were
well above head height. A beekeeper, who had worked one of the
trees as late as the 1920s, gave us a vivid account of the hazards
involved. In the New Forest the bee trees had to be worked
surreptitiously, because both land and trees (and consequently
the honey) were in the ownership of the Crown. So the tell-tale
door had to be camouflaged with bark.

In many places hives as separate and movable containers for
bees were adapted from containers used for other purposes, or
containers were simply adopted as they were. Most materials
used – wood, reeds, wicker, straw, clay – would have provided
fairly good thermal insulation. I do not think metal was ever
used; a so-called bronze hive from Pompeii, which is often
referred to, was neither a hive nor made of bronze. Baskets for
carrying agricultural materials, and water pots, were often of a
size acceptable to a swarm of bees for a nesting place.

As a general rule hives were placed upright in the region north
of the mountain ranges that stretch across Europe and Asia from
the Iberian peninsula to Kamchatka, and horizontally everywhere else. For instance hewn-out log hives were stood upright in
Russia, but are used horizontally in tropical Africa. Elongated
wicker skeps are used on their side in Mali today (one is
portrayed on the gourd in the cover illustration), and these are
hardly distinguishable from some of the wicker skeps used
vertically in medieval Europe. Clay cylinders are used vertically
in Portugal, but horizontally throughout North Africa.

Hives in any one area were made of local materials using local
techniques; if other vessels were adapted for use as hives, they
might only be changed slightly, for instance to provide for a flight

22. Two wicker skeps on a bench, with one of the earliest depictions of a beekeeper wearing protective clothing, from Sebastian Münster, *Cosmographia*, Basel, 1544.

entrance, or a roof. What is astonishing is the lack of change in these hives, over centuries and even millennia. Hives similar to those portrayed in 1450 BC (fig. 20) can be found in Egypt today. Wicker and straw skeps, where they are still in use, are little changed from the earliest representations known. Archaeologists are now starting to recognize fragments of beehives among coarse pottery sherds they find, and we are learning that hives used in Ancient Greece have counterparts among hives still in use in Mediterranean countries. Two of the best-preserved examples of Ancient Greek horizontal clay hives had been used mouth-to-mouth to form a coffin for a ten-year-old boy*. The unchanging nature of the hives is partly due to the unchanging demand made of them: the bees were killed to get the honey, and as long as this practice continued no advance in design was called for.

* I am indebted to Dr. A. J. Graham for news of this recent find.

23. 'Hiving a swarm', a wicker hive in use in England, from F.G. Jenyns, *A book about bees*, 1886.

Hives in the IBRA Collection of Beekeeping Material exemplify the wide variety of local materials and crafts used in different parts of the world for making hives. The most primitive is an egg-shaped hive made of mud, straw and cow dung, still used in the High Simien Mountains of Ethiopia. Fired clay pots come from countries and islands of the eastern and southern Mediterranean. Woven cane cylinders come from China and Ethiopia, and woven wicker hives (skeps) from England, Belgium and Luxembourg, and also West Africa. Coiled straw skeps were in recent use in Britain, France, Germany, Belgium and the Netherlands. Examples of hewn wooden hives come from the Arabian peninsula, East Africa and the USA, and splendid bark hives from Tanzania. Upright cork hives are used in the Iberian peninsula, and similar hives are used horizontally in Algeria. A hive from Bali in Indonesia, used for *Apis cerana*, is made from the shells, leaves and parts of flowers of the coconut, and gourds are used as hives for stingless bees in Brazil and Mexico. All these types of hive could have been made and used in Bronze Age times; many may have existed much earlier. All have been found still in use since 1960.

Initially such hives as these were worked for honey as wild colonies were. Once a year, the hive was opened, usually at a point distant from the flight hole, or a basket was lifted off its base and upturned. The bees were driven out of the hive by smoke, or suffocated, or drowned by immersing the hive in water. Combs were then broken or cut out, in later times with a specially designed knife. When clothes were worn, the beekeeper did what he could to protect himself from stinging by covering his face as well as his body, but stings were an occupational hazard, and accepted as part of the price paid for the prize to be gained. The combs were put into a container, and might be strained through woven fibre or cloth (a 'honey poke' in England). The residue in the straining bag would often be put into water to make mead, and the wax rendered for making candles, polishes and ointments.

In the tropics the empty hives could be left in position for swarms from other colonies to occupy in due course. In temperate regions some colonies had to be kept over the winter to provide next year's stock; a common custom was to kill off the heaviest colonies (yielding most honey) and the lightest (least likely to survive until spring), and to overwinter the medium ones, leaving their honey in the hives. The method most often described for killing the bees was setting the hive over a hole dug in the ground, in which sulphur-impregnated papers were burned. This was not done without remorse, as is shown by the following extract from Anne Hughes's *The diary of a farmer's wife 1796–1797*:

It do grieve me to kill the poor things, being such a waste of good bees, to lie in a great heap at the bottom of the hole when the skep be took off it, but we do want the honey, using a great lot in the house for divers times ... We shall break the honey combs up and hang it up in a clean cotton bag to run it through then we shall strain it divers times and when clear put the pots reddie to use. The wax we do boil many times till it be a nice yaller colour and no bits of black in it, when it can be stored for use for the polishing and harness cleaning.

(serialized in *Farmer's Weekly* 1937; first published in book form by Countryside Books 1964.)

HONEY IN EVERYDAY LIFE

George Duby's *Rural Economy and Country Life in the Medieval West* (Edward Arnold, 1968) provides interesting evidence on rural economy in medieval Europe and helps us to see the importance of honey in the general pattern of life. An inventory made on the border of Flanders about AD 800 mentioned 'a little courtyard surrounded by a hedge, well ordered and planted with trees of different kinds' where perhaps bees were kept, and 'from the four gardens three muids of honey were offered'.*

A contemporary inventory of a Bavarian abbey with 72 prebendaries included 63 geese, 50 chickens and 17 beehives, also half a measure of honey and 2 of butter. A lord's manse near Rheims had 87 geese, 44 ganders, 157 hens, 182 chicks and 21 beehives. In 840 Abbot Einhard, Charlemagne's biographer, sent a message to the agent at his demesne at St. Bavo in Ghent: 'We have need of wax for our use and we cannot procure any here because the honey harvest has been small these last two years in the country.'

In 1080–1082 monks of St. Aubin of Angers extracted tolls on commodities peddled by peasants in neighbouring markets. Tolls were not payable for what was carried on the neck, except for feathers (1 denier); wax (honeycomb a halfpenny); a hive (a halfpenny); lard (a ham with its lard 1 denier); a bed with bedding (1 denier); a wedding outfit (4 deniers) ... An ox, ass or pig, like a hive, was charged a halfpenny.

In England in the 1400s, a hive from which honey was taken every other year was expected to yield 2 gallons (say 30 lb, 14 kg). In the mid-1500s a charcoal burner in Essex sold his landlord 2 gallons of honey for 65d (old pence), at a time when pigeons were 18d for 12 and geese 5d each. In general the larger households produced the honey they used, and for this reason honey is not often found in early records of household expenditure.

Entries in wills give some idea of the number of hives held, and how they and their honey were regarded. The following from Essex were found by F. G. Emmison:

---

* The muid varied from place to place; in Paris it was 268 litres, and three muids of honey there would weigh more than a ton.

1570   Romford man named Empsall: 'to my dame a swarm of bees
      which I have at Noak Hill'
      John Dyer, husbandman: 'eleven hives'

1584   William Styleman, yeoman: 6 of 10 hives with bees to his
      maidservant and 1 to his vicar

1593   Roger Huen: his stock of bees to his son, except 12 hives to his
      wife.

Other entries refer to 9 stocks of bees; 4 skeps or hives of bees; 4
hives and a swarm (distributed by a widow among five friends); 'a
pot of honey and a hive of bees' and 'all my bees with their hives
and honey'.

In 1563 Margery, widow of Tristram Cooke of Romford, willed
on her deathbed that her daughter Elizabeth 'be in the keeping of
Mrs. Flouere' and that 'my executor do array her handsomely
and deliver a cow with her to her said mistress and two hives with
bees'. In the above entries a swarm would be a (young) colony,
and a person's stock of bees would mean all his hives with the
bees in them.

In the Middle Ages it was not uncommon for hives of bees to
be left to a church, to provide beeswax for candles. For instance
in 1407 Henry Castilay of Bexley in Kent ordered that he should
be buried in Bexley Church, and that mass should be said there
daily for two years for the repose of his soul; he bequeathed all his
bees to the churchwardens of Bexley, the profit from them to be
devoted towards maintaining three wax tapers in the church, ever
burning, one before St. Mary in the chancel, another before St.
Catherine, and the third before St. Margaret.

After the dissolution of the monasteries in the 1520s and 1530s
the practice probably dwindled, but in 1558, the last year of the
reign of the Roman Catholic Queen Mary, it was recorded in the
churchwardens' accounts at the parish church of Cheswardine in
Shropshire that Christopher Virges 'will give or bequeathe a
swarm of bees to maintain a light or candle before or in front of
the Image or Statue of St. Katherine'.

An almost contemporary will, made by John Howkie of
Holdenhurst near Bournemouth in Hampshire in 1560, includes
the dispositions of his four apiaries:

Item. I give and bequethe to Joan Howkie my wiffe and to John Howkie
my sonne my garden of hyves and I will that the said Joan and John my

sonne shall have the benefit and increase of the said garden between them as long as the said Joan shall continue to be alive or do marrie if the said Joan my wiffe do depart this world or do marrie then I will that the whole garden of hyves remayne fully and holy to John Howkie my sonne.

Item. I gyve to Thomas Howkie my sonne all my hyves in the handes of Thomas Mann.

Item. I gyve to Richard Howkie my sonne all my hyves with Hewgh Warne.

Item. I gyve to Margaret my daughter half my hyves now in the handes of Edward Barone and the other half to the said Edward Barone himself.

But not all was sweetness and light where bees and honey were concerned. In 1654 there was a presentment to Hertfordshire County Sessions that Thomas Worlands, of Ashwell, did 'take away one hive of bees' the property of James Bowne. At Bedfordshire Quarter Sessions in 1742 Edmond Bate was charged with stealing one beehive, and in 1808 Edward Dowdeswell of Maulden, victualler, gave information that 'on Monday morning last he missed two hives of Bees with the honey from his garden, and found a quantity of honey and the comb in the house of Thomas Young, of Maulden'. In 1809 the same Thomas Young, labourer, was indicted for stealing 'two stocks of bees, value 10 shillings, six pounds of honey, value 5 shillings, one pound of bees-wax, value 10 pence, two straw bee hives, value 1 shilling.' There is no record of his sentence, but on 10 January of the same year the General Quarter Sessions at Reading in Berkshire found John Bristow guilty of stealing two hives of bees belonging to Wm. Money of Waltham St. Lawrence, and sentenced him to be transported for seven years. (At the same Sessions Wm. Hicks was sentenced to one month's imprisonment for stealing bread out of a cart.) John Bristow would have fared even worse in the Isle of Man, where it was a capital offence to steal bees. A Manx law passed in 1629, and not repealed until 1817, laid down that 'the stealing and cutting of Beehives in Gardens shall be Fellony in like manner to death, without valuing the same'.

Bees and honey were valuable, and so was sugar until the last century. As 'the honey from reeds', it had been known throughout antiquity, and sugar cane seems to have been introduced to southern China around 200 BC. It was regarded as an expensive sort of 'concreted' honey, and was used for medicinal purposes only. The Arabs cultivated and processed sugar (the word comes from the Arabic *sukkar*), but it was not much used in Europe until the period of Islamic influence in the 1100s. An early English reference is in the Bishop of Hereford's household roll for 1289, where sugar was grouped with the similarly expensive spices. The early 1600s saw the start of the sugar cane plantations in the West Indies, and these islands thereafter became the main source of supply for the European and American markets.

We can compare prices in England for honey and white sugar in the 1400s and 1500s. Honey averaged 1·17d a pound in 1410, and the rare and costly imported sugar 24d a pound. By 1490, with honey still at 1·15d, sugar had dropped to 6·50d; in 1530 they were 1·64d and 6·75d, but by 1580 inflation had taken them to 3·40d and 17·23d. White sugar was still a rich man's luxury. Sugar and honey reached parity in the 1800s, and since then honey has been the dearer. Figures published in 1965 show the relationship between the retail prices of honey and sugar in ten countries. In the USA honey was 1½ times as expensive as sugar, in France, Romania and USSR 2 to 3 times, in Czechoslovakia, England, Greece and Sweden 3 to 4 times, and in Austria and the German Federal Republic 5 to 6 times.

The 'explosion' of sugar production and consumption came after 1700; in England the annual consumption rose 15-fold between 1700 and 1800. By 1850 world consumption was 1½ million tons, by 1890 over 5, by 1900 11, by 1950 35, and by 1972 over 70 million tons – a 50-fold increase in 150 years.

The UK has better long-term statistics than any other country, and from them we learn that just over 200 years ago the annual sugar consumption was around 2 kg per capita; now it is over 50 kg. A level of 2 kg could well have matched the honey consumption in the Middle Ages. It is commonly said that honey was then 'the only sweetener' for most people, but sweetness was not at all a common characteristic of foods. The present high consumption of sweet foods and drinks in many countries is a concomitant of the growth of the sugar industry, and has little to do with honey.

BETTER TIMES FOR THE BEES

Although it was a common practice to kill a colony of bees in order to take its honey, better methods had been used by the more knowledgeable beekeepers since ancient times. Such methods were, however, unfamiliar enough to make news right up to the last century. The principle was to remove honey combs that lay outside the brood nest, which was left more or less intact with its bees, brood and queen, so that the colony lived on. One French account of (horizontal) hives used in Ethiopia explained the necessity of making them longer than a man's arm-reach by the length of his hand, so that when the beekeeper reached into the hive to take out the combs, he was forced to leave enough behind for the colony to survive. As he would first have smoked the bees to the far end of the hive, the queen and many bees would, with luck, have been driven beyond his reach.

James Boswell, the biographer of Samuel Johnson, was interested in seeing that honey could be harvested without killing the bees. On 17 October 1765, when he stayed for two nights in the Franciscan convent at Corte in Corsica, he made the following entry in his journal:

These fathers have a good vineyard and an excellent garden. They have between thirty and forty beehives in long wooden cases or trunks of trees, with a covering of the bark of the cork tree. When they want honey they burn a little juniper wood, the smoke of which makes the bees retire. They then take an iron instrument with a sharp-edged crook at one end of it and bring out the greatest part of the honeycomb, leaving only a little for the bees, who work the case full again. By taking the honey in this way they never kill a bee.

The diarist Samuel Pepys, already quoted in Chapter 4, wrote on 5 May 1665:

After dinner, to Mr. Evelyn's; he being abroad, we walked in his garden [at Deptford], and a lovely noble ground he hath indeed. And, among other rarities, a hive of bees, so as, being hived in glass, you may see the bees making their honey and combs mighty pleasantly.

Meanwhile, bees had been given new foraging grounds, in the New World, to which they were first taken by settlers from the Old World in and after the 1600s. We may never know the date and the circumstances in which honeybees first survived the

Atlantic crossing. The earliest likely record that has come to light is in a letter dated 5 December 1621 from the Council of the Virginia Company in London to the Governor and Council in Virginia: 'We have by this Ship [either the *Bona Nova* or the *Hopewell*] and the *Discovery* sent you divers sorte of seed, and fruit trees, as also Pidgeons, Connies [rabbits], Peacocke maistives [mastiffs], and Beehives.' There is unfortunately no mention of the arrival of the bees.

In many of the places to which the bees were taken, they survived the winters and prospered sufficiently to yield honey for their owners, and to throw swarms – which spread in advance of the settlers. The bees were called 'white man's flies' by the American Indians, and were justifiably dreaded as heralding the arrival of pale-face intruders; white clover, which spread similarly, was known as the 'white man's foot':

> Whereso'er they move, before them
> Swarms the stinging fly, the Ahmo,
> Swarms the Bee, the honey-maker;
> Wheresoe'er they tread, beneath them
> Springs a flower unknown among us,
> Springs the White Man's Foot in blossom.
>
> *Hiawatha* by H. W. Longfellow (1855)

Bees had probably become fairly common throughout the eastern part of North America by 1800. The first honeybees were landed in Australia in 1810. W. C. Cotton took a consignment to New Zealand in 1842, but an even earlier record has now come to light. In March 1839 Mary Anna Bumby, sister of a missionary, landed at Mungunga (North Island) with two straw skeps of black bees she had brought from England. They were placed in the mission churchyard, which was 'considered the most free from possible disturbance through the curiosity of the Natives, who had never previously seen the bee'.

THE REVOLUTION IN HONEY PRODUCTION

Attempts to improve existing systems of beekeeping had been intensified in the 1600s, partly from the spirit of enquiry that was abroad at the time, and partly on humanitarian and economic grounds; this is summed up in the passage already quoted from

The diary of a farmer's wife: 'it *do grieve me* to kill the poor things, being *such a waste* of good bees'. The 'never kill a bee' movement spread especially in the 1820s, through such books as Thomas Nutt's *Humanity to honey bees* (1832) and *A short and simple letter to cottagers* (1839) – by 'A bee preserver' (in fact W. C. Cotton).

The experimenting and the discussions had continued for some 200 years, but still without much advance being made. Providing the hive with an extension in which the bees stored honey, and which could then be removed after the bees had been driven out to re-enter the hive itself, gave a partial solution. The honey in the extension (the honey chamber) was generally cleaner and, being in new combs, more delicate to eat. The hive extension might be a cap or a bell jar placed above a skep, the flat top of which had a hole to provide a passage way; or a shallow cylindrical ring called an *eke* placed under a skep of the same diameter; or wooden boxes fixed at the side of a wooden box hive, passage ways being provided between the several parts of this so-called eclectic hive. There was a sale to the quality trade of the honey chambers full of comb – ready packaged merchandize, that saved the producer much work in separating the honey from the comb.

These hives still gave the beekeeper almost no control over the central part of the hive, where the brood was reared. To remove a comb he had to cut it out, and he could not then replace it. The reason for this was that the bees built their combs downwards from the top of the hive, which had to be solid enough to support them. A considerable breakthrough came when bar hives of various kinds were invented: parallel bars of wood were supported across an inner hive top, at the same distance apart as naturally built combs. But the bees still attached their combs to the hive at the sides. The experimenters then learned that bees would 'respect' a bee-space – as between two opposite comb surfaces, for instance – and not build comb across it. The final advance was made by the Rev. L. L. Langstroth in Philadelphia, USA, in 1851: he extended the top-bar down at its two ends to make a frame. If the ends of the frame were kept at a bee-space distance from the inner hive walls, the bees did not build comb across the gap, and the frame was removable. Langstroth was one who could express his ideas on paper, and his book *The hive and the honeybee* (1853 and many subsequent editions) spread the gospel of 'rational' beekeeping throughout the world. As T.W. Cowan, doyen of English beekeeping, wrote on Langstroth's death in 1895:

The opening of the hive at the top, the perfect interchangeability of the movable combs, and the lateral movement of the frames, have given the beekeeper the most perfect control over his bees, and have more than justified Langstroth's expectations when he wrote the note in his diary in 1851, that 'The use of these frames will, I am persuaded, give a new impetus to the easy and profitable management of bees'.

For advanced beekeepers in different parts of the world, the time was ripe for an expedient that would release them from the bondage of immovable combs. Many different movable-frame hives were developed in various countries, but the type following directly from Langstroth's, and called the Langstroth hive, is more widely used than any other in the world today.

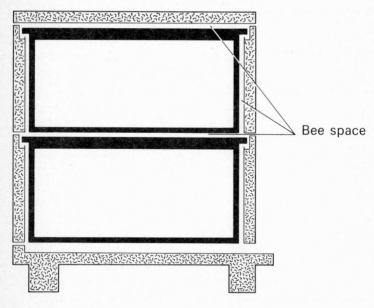

Bee space

24. Section through a movable-frame hive showing suspended frames in place. The hive shown has two boxes/chambers/bodies; a queen excluder inserted between them would define the lower one as a brood chamber and the upper one as a honey chamber.

The movable-frame hive (fig. 24) was followed by the invention of embossed beeswax 'foundation' to fit into the frames; by the centrifugal extractor that spun the honey out of them, leaving the strengthened framed combs ready for re-use; and by the queen excluder, a grid to separate the brood chamber from the honey chamber, penetrable by workers but not by the queen. Inventions have multiplied, but there are not many fields of activity where there is such a clear-cut division between the old and traditional and the new and rational. Florence Naile's 1942 biography of Langstroth was reprinted in 1976 with a foreword by Dr. R. A. Morse, which includes the tribute:

Few industries can point to one man, or pinpoint a single date in their histories, and say, 'This was the beginning'. The beekeeping industry is an exception ... It is possible that Langstroth's greatest contribution to beekeeping was his book ... first published in 1853. Langstroth not only revealed his discoveries to the world, but also, and more importantly, gave sound, practical advice on bee management. Without his writings the world might have known little about the principle of bee space and its implications for beekeeping.

What Langstroth's development made possible was the manipulation of a colony of bees so that it produced honey greatly in excess of its requirements – the colony could overwinter, and the beekeeper could get his harvest as well. This manipulation is, basically:

1. the colony winters with enough stores (checked by the bee-keeper), in a hive of a suitable size;
2. in spring, honey chambers (*supers*) are superimposed on the brood chamber (above a queen excluder) one by one as the colony expands, so that – ideally – the colony continues to grow but is never crowded enough to swarm; if necessary more brood space is provided as well;
3. the colony, not having swarmed, has a very large force of foraging bees for the main honey flow, and accumulates considerably more honey than it needs for the next winter.

In nature the colony would have reproduced by swarming at stage 2, leaving two colonies by the end of the season, each with some honey, but the beekeeper would get hardly any unless he killed a colony to get it. Honey production for the beekeeper is an alternative to reproduction of the colony by swarming.

In terms of real money, these technological developments have made honey cheaper, although fluctuations in the price of honey, as of other world commodities, are still governed by world economic trends and crises. From 1880 to 1914 the price of honey sold to dealers in New York was steady at 5 to 9 cents a lb. As a result of World War I it rose to 26 cents a lb by 1920, but it dropped to 11 cents in the next two years. The price then remained steady until 1941 (except for a drop to 5 cents in 1933, during the slump), rose during World War II to 25 cents in 1947, and steadied at 16 to 19 cents during the years up to 1971. Then, poor crops in the main exporting countries, coupled with increasing world demand, pushed the price up to 51 cents by 1975.

HONEY AS A WORLD COMMODITY

Now, more than a century after the inception of the movable-frame hive, honey is produced in almost every country of the world, and is an article of commerce within the country and often with other countries as well.

The annual world production of honey is around 800,000 tons, of which over half is produced in the three largest beekeeping countries: the USA, USSR, and the People's Republic of China. The production by continent is given in Appendix 2 (Table 14). The profitability of honey production in an area may be assessed roughly by the annual honey yield per colony; if this yield is high, beekeepers are likely to be making their living from honey production rather than keeping bees as a hobby or as a sideline, and the number of colonies per beekeeper will be high. There are many complicating factors, but the following examples illustrate this relationship. Canada, Australia and Israel all produce an average of at least 40 kg per hive, and the average holding is 37 colonies or more per beekeeper. Argentina and New Zealand produce around 20–30 kg per hive, and the average holding is 30 hives. The German Federal Republic, the Netherlands and Switzerland, however, produce 10 kg or less per hive, and the average holding is 7–12 hives, most beekeepers in these countries being hobbyists or part-timers.

Of the 800,000 tons produced each year, over 600,000 tons are consumed in the country of origin, and 150,000 tons exported.

New World countries dominate the export trade, whereas all the main honey imports are into Old World countries. Two-thirds of the world's honey exports are from Mexico, the People's Republic of China, Argentina and Australia, and about the same amount is imported into the world's great honey-importing countries, the German Federal Republic, the UK and Japan.

The honey that is exported is generally surplus to the requirements of the countries producing it, although what counts as surplus in any one country may be determined on a political rather than a nutritional or gastronomic basis. We must delve deeper to discover why people of some nationalities eat far more honey than they can produce; why some produce a lot and eat all of it (or almost none); and why still others produce very little, although bees can thrive and honey-yielding plants are available. These are human problems rather than bee problems.

Most people are conservative in what they like to eat, and this is especially true of geographical or ethnic groups who can reinforce individual preferences by social custom. Traditionally, for the past thousand years or more at any rate, honey has been part of the diet of central and north-west European people especially. Today honey consumption is relatively high in these same parts of Europe, and in the parts of other continents settled by these Europeans.

The world average consumption per person each year is about 0·17 kg of honey, compared with 20 kg of sugar, but there are wide and interesting variations.

Both sugar and honey consumption are highest in Europe and countries settled from there, including Canada, the USA, Australia, New Zealand, Israel, and the Soviet Union: sugar over 20 kg (sometimes over 40 kg) and honey over 500 g. (In Canada, between 1970 and 1975 the honey consumption per person increased by about 10 per cent, whereas that of other sugar products dropped by 18 per cent.) This group includes many of the most affluent countries in the world: Sweden, Switzerland, the German Federal Republic, the USA, Canada, Australia, New Zealand. It may be significant that, except for Israel, inhabitants of the countries outside Europe with a high honey consumption are all primarily of Anglo-Saxon origin.

Sugar and honey consumption are rather less high, but in

similar proportions, in countries of southern Europe (Italy, Portugal, Spain, etc.) and in two countries settled from there (Argentina and Uruguay) that are too far south to grow sugar – and also in Japan, discussed below.

There are other high sugar-eating countries in tropical and subtropical Latin America where sugar is grown, but in these countries honey is an insignificant part of the diet. In Cuba sugar consumption is 78 kg per head per year. Mexico and Brazil are medium sugar eaters, but low honey eaters.

It is thus clear that if people want to eat honey and cannot produce it, they import it (for example Germany), but the fact that people produce much honey does not make them eat honey (for example Mexico), nor does high sugar consumption imply high honey consumption (for example Cuba).

In many countries of Asia, very little sugar *or* honey is eaten. Sugar figures are available for China and Sri Lanka as 4 kg a year, and for India and Indonesia as 6 kg; the honey consumption is estimated as only 2–3 g in China and India, and is not likely to be higher in the other two countries. Israel and Japan are among the exceptions. Until after World War II Japan conformed to the habits of other Asiatic countries in eating little sugar or honey, but it has since moved in a startling fashion towards a Western diet, and has been converted to sweetness in foods. (I do not know of a people that has been weaned from it.) The sugar and honey consumption of Japan has become more like that of North America and Western Europe, and Japan is now a major honey-importing country.

The African continent shares with Europe a long tradition of honey-getting. Of the known rock paintings that show scenes related to bees or honey hunting, a few are in Spain (fig. 18) and the rest – nearly a hundred – in Africa (fig. 17). One is known in India (fig. 19). Data on sugar and honey consumption in Africa are few and frail. On average not more than 15 kg of sugar are currently consumed per person per year, together with several kg of honey. The people have not, however, been in the habit of *eating* so much honey: the men consume much of it converted into alcohol, in honey beer. Ethiopia is one country where this drink (*tej*) is very common indeed, although only in the Christian areas, alcohol being forbidden to the Muslims.

Because honey keeps and travels well, it can be harvested from hives in the good honey-producing countries and exported to the rest of the world, where it is valued as a delicacy and purchased by those who can afford it: it is a food of the more affluent societies. Side by side with the status of honey as a world commodity, there is the fact that honey just taken from the hive is at its highest excellence. This is one of the reasons why beekeepers in every country believe that home-produced honey is best.

6. Bees and honey in the minds of men

BEFORE RECORDED HISTORY: HONEY AND BEES ARE MIRACULOUS

The early part of this book is concerned with facts – about the plants honey comes from, the bees that make it, and the honey itself. Most were discovered only within the present century, and were thus unknown to all but the last few generations of mankind that have eaten honey for sustenance or pleasure. Then Chapter 5 follows the history of honey in people's everyday life. In this chapter we shall trace the parallel development of honey, and of bees, as they have appeared in the minds of men through succeeding ages. We shall be dealing with beliefs and ideas rather than with facts, but beliefs can influence men's actions more than facts do, so the subject is important. It is also of unusual interest.

We have seen in Chapter 5 that honey was a valued food from the very beginning of man's existence: worth hunting for, and even worth the suffering caused by inevitable bee stings. It is less easy to see what, if anything, honey meant to earliest man apart from food, but there are several clues: in languages, and in writings that are based on early oral tradition, and in drawings made by prehistoric peoples. It is likely that honey was one of the things people talked about soon after they could express their thoughts in words. The evidence for this is the fact that the words for *honey* in widely different languages are quite remarkably similar, indicating that honey was known by name at a very early stage in the development of human language. This is also true for the words for *mead*, the alcoholic drink from honey, and somewhat less so for the words for *bee*, suggesting that the insect producing the honey was not named until later.

Except in Germanic languages, the various Indo-European words for honey are derived from only two primeval terms:

medhu- and *melit-*, so the word-roots in the many different languages must have been formed before the languages became separated. *Medhu-* occurs in virtually all Indo-European languages; some of its descendants denote both *mead* and *honey*, others *mead* only, in which case *honey* is denoted by a derivation of *melit-*. Hittite had *milit*, Sanskrit *madhu*. Outside the Indo-European group, *medhu-* has led to Hungarian *mez* and Finnish *mesi* (nectar); it is possible that the word for honey in some oriental languages is also derived from *medhu-*, via Tocharian *mit*; for instance Japanese *mitsu*, Chinese *mi* and Sino-Korean *mil*.

In the extreme west of Europe, the Celtic languages have retained different derivatives for *honey* and *mead*: Welsh *mel*, *medd*; Breton *mel*, *mez*; Cornish *mel*, *meth*; Irish *mil*, *miodh*; but Scottish Gaelic *mil* only. Gothic retained both words, but the Germanic languages derived from it replaced *milith-* by a word something like *hunaga*, meaning gold or yellow. From this came Old Norse *hunang*, German *Honig*, Old English *hunig*, and so on.

The wider distribution of *medhu-*, the root word for mead, than of *melit-* meaning honey only, seems to suggest that mead from fermented honey was relished even earlier than the honey itself. Mead is an alcoholic drink that could easily be produced without man's deliberate agency – when a bees' nest was flooded, or when rain had filled a vessel containing broken honeycombs, for instance. Several Greek legends refer to the time before wine was known, when mead was the only intoxicant. If this time covered a long period in prehistory, it would help to account for some of the magical properties attributed to honey, which we shall now explore.

The most extensive line of evidence is to be found in beliefs, rites and customs that have survived to the present day, by usage and oral transmission in primitive societies and also in writings recovered from some more advanced cultures. Where a belief or custom has been found across the whole of the Indo-European region, and also in eastern Asia and in Africa, it seems reasonable to assume that it dates from a very early prehistoric era. By piecing together such evidence, we are able to get a glimmering of insight into the minds of early men and women.

Studies of the place of honey in early societies were published by various German authors from the 1890s to the 1930s. I am indebted also to three publications in English: Hilda M. Ransome's book *The sacred bee* (1937), Dr. B. F. Beck's book *Honey and health* (1938), and Austin E. Fife's doctorate thesis *The concept of the sacredness of bees, honey and wax in Christian popular tradition* (Stanford University, USA, 1939). Dr. Fife's synthesis enlightens a vast mass of isolated records by abandoning the geographical approach favoured earlier and seeking the underlying links between them. In what follows I have also incorporated other information not available to these authors.

Just as the word for honey is older than the word for bee, so honey was regarded as sacred before bees were – honey was the valued food, bees just got in the way. Early man guessed that bees somehow obtained honey from flowers and trees, but it was not until the 1700s that anyone realized that flowers themselves *produced* the nectar that bees collected. Until that time it had been assumed that nectar (or honeydew) fell from the air; it was an exudation from heaven, and hence a food of both gods and men, and set apart from all other foods. In the first century BC Aristotle put it thus: 'Honey falls from the air, principally at the rising of the stars, and when the rainbow rests upon the earth' (*Historia animalium* V, 22–24), to which Pliny the Elder added: 'Whether it is that this liquid is the sweet of the heavens, or whether a saliva emanating from the stars, or a juice exuding from the air while purifying itself ... it comes to us pure, limpid and genuine' (*Historia naturalis* XI, 12).

There was not much enlightenment in the next 1,600 years; Charles Butler's *Feminine monarchie*, published in 1609, which was the best beekeeping book of its period, had not advanced noticeably on the ideas of Aristotle and Pliny:

The greatest plenty of purest nectar cometh from above; which Almighty God doth miraculously distil out of the air ... What this *mel rosidum* should be, Pliny seemeth much in doubt. But, if conjectures might be admitted, I would rather judge it to be the very quintessence of all the sweetness of the earth (which at that time is most plentiful) drawn up, as other dews, in vapours into the lowest region of the air, by the exceeding and continual heat of the sun; and there concreted and condensated by the nightly cold into this most sweet and sovereign nectar, which thence doth descend into the earth in a dew or small drizzling rain.

There are many specific references in early classical literature to honey as the food of a god and to mead as his drink; alternative words were ambrosia and nectar, or vice versa. In ancient literature – and also in more recent poetry – the word honeydew was used similarly, as by Coleridge in *Kubla Khan*:

> For he on honey-dew hath fed
> And drunk the milk of Paradise.

In apicultural circles, however, honeydew nowadays denotes an aphid secretion on plants.

Honey, of divine origin and the food of the gods, became associated early with Paradise in the world to come, the Isles of the Blest; whatever name was used, recurrent features were streams flowing with milk and honey, honey in every flower, a spring of honey, a well of mead ...

Since honey was the food of the gods, it must be sacrificed to gods, and it was in fact one of the most universal of all sacrifices, offered by many peoples, including those of Sumeria, Babylon, India, Egypt, Greece and Rome, northern Europe, Africa and Central America. Dr. Beck recognized that honey was universally used in consecratory rites when people wished to offer something especially holy and acceptable to a deity, as an expression of thanksgiving, penitence or atonement. Hilda Ransome was struck by the fact that the rites using honey belonged to the earliest cults, those of the spirits of the dead, of the underworld deities, and of snakes. Many of them went back into the dim ages when the only intoxicant was a drink made by fermenting honey.

The long list of principal gods to whom the Greeks and Romans sacrificed honey included especially those concerned with the productiveness of nature, for instance Artemis, Ceres, Persephone, Aphrodite, Dionysus, Bacchus, Apollo and Pluto. Fertility, abundance (in both plant and animal kingdoms), and love – with feminine beauty also – were the aspects of worship in which honey was particularly involved. By good chance records have survived of some of the quantities of honey sacrificed in Ancient Egypt; one list of offerings made by Rameses III (1198–1167 BC) to the Nile god amounts to about fifteen tons of honey. This implies that beekeeping was practised on quite a large scale.

Another series of rites dependent on honey was so universal

that it must also be very old: those marking important personal events associated with the renewal of life – birth, marriage, and death, which was the entry into afterlife. The practice of giving honey to a child after birth was at least as widespread as the use of honey as a sacrificial offering, and is prehistoric in origin. It may well be that honey was first chosen as a child's initial food, even before mother's milk, because of its acceptability. But the practice came to be associated with the cult of the divine nature of honey, and the belief arose that honey had the mysterious power of protecting the child from evil spirits and demons.

One of the best-known legends concerns the infant Zeus, concealed in a cave in Mount Dicte in Crete by his mother Rhea to save him from his father Kronos, who had killed their previous five children. In the cave the goat Amaltheia fed him with milk, and sacred bees (or nymphs) fed him with honey. On one occasion honey hunters entered the sacred cave, wearing their armour against expected stings. But, when they started to take the honey from the bees' nest, they saw the infant Zeus in his swaddling clothes; at this sight their armour burst and fell off, leaving them unprotected against the sacred bees. On a Greek amphora from 550 BC in the British Museum (*Catalogue of Vases* II, B177), there is an entertaining picture of the bees attacking the naked men.

In marriage ceremonies, the use of honey occurs constantly in the entire Indo-European region and among many peoples outside it. Honey seems to have been a symbol of the sweetness of love in prehistoric times, as in every age since, and the poetry of people all over the world compares the sweetness of love with honey. (The ancient Indian god of love, Kama, carried a bow whose string was made of a chain of bees.*)

The word *honeymoon*, however, probably carries no more significance than that the first month of marriage is the sweetest; it does not refer to a month-long feasting on honey. In the marriage ceremony itself honey was, and is, used variously as a gift, for eating, for drinking as mead, and for anointing, and smearing on the lintel and door posts of the new home.

Honey is as universally attested in death rites as in those of

* Fife strongly rejects the idea that these bees symbolize the pain of love, regarding the whole concept of the bitter-sweetness of love as a sophisticated notion indicating 'an advanced and very civilized analysis of the psychology of love'.

birth and marriage. In addition to its use in sacrificial rituals and as food for the dead, honey has another important property: it is a very good preservative for a corpse, and was possibly the only one available in prehistoric and early historical times. In the Ancient World honey was widely used in embalming; the body of Achilles was laid 'in the clothing of the gods, in lavish unguents and sweet honey' (*Odyssey* XXIV, 68). We learn from Strabo that the body of Alexander the Great, on his own order, was placed in white honey in a golden coffin. Herod I, King of Judaea, who had his beautiful wife Mariamne executed, then kept her body for seven years preserved in honey, 'for he loved her even in death'.

A number of the rites already referred to may be regarded as purification ceremonies, and honey was also consistently used in rites where purification was the primary purpose. In the Mithraic cult, for instance, honey was poured on the hands instead of water, to keep them pure and undefiled. Honey was used together with milk (or butter, curds, or ghee) for various purposes: in consecrating priests and priestesses, exorcising evil spirits, consecrating temples, and as the sacred food of initiates in various religions. More than this, the two foods together were a widely used symbol of riches and plenty; in the Old Testament there are no fewer than twenty-one references to the Promised Land as 'flowing with milk and honey'.

Man's earliest concern for bees was entirely secondary to his interest in honey. But as he became interested in bees in their own right, they seemed most mysterious and therefore magical creatures. Singly the bees flew out and home again; more astonishingly, at a certain season they flew out as a swarm that seemed to have a mind of its own. They showed miraculous fertility: after the end of a dearth period when growth had been halted, a handful of bees would increase their number in a short time to a swirling mass, yet their method of generation could not be seen or understood, as could that of mammals and birds. Even the great Aristotle, with his exceptional grasp of natural phenomena, had to confess that 'there is much difficulty about the generation of bees'. Extracts from his proposals and counter-proposals are as follows:

For they must (1) either bring the young brood from elsewhere, as some say, and if so the young must either be spontaneously generated or produced by some other animal, or (2) they must generate them themselves, or (3) they must bring some and generate others, for this also is maintained by some, who say that they bring the young of the drones only. Again, if they generate them it must be either with or without copulation; if the former, then either (1) each kind must generate its own kind, or (2) some one kind must generate the others, or (3) one kind must unite with another for the purpose. (I mean for instance (1) that bees may be generated from the union of bees, drones from that of drones, and kings from that of kings, or (2) that all the others may be generated from one, as from what are called kings and leaders, or (3) from the union of drones and bees, for some say that the former are male, the latter female, while others say that the bees are male and the drones female.) ... That they should collect honey is reasonable, for it is their food, but it is strange that they should collect the young if they are neither their own offspring nor food ... But, again, it is also unreasonable to suppose that the bees are female and the drones male, for Nature does not give weapons for fighting to any female, and while the drones are stingless all the bees have a sting. Nor is the opposite view reasonable, that the bees are male and the drones female, for no males are in the habit of working for their offspring ... And an argument against both theories, that the young are generated by union of the bees with one another or with the drones, separately or with one another, is this: none of them has ever yet been seen copulating, whereas this would have often happened if the sexes had existed in them.

De generatione animalium 10, 759a,b.

To primitive man, therefore, bees were a supreme example of the miraculous creative power of Nature, and the bees themselves were miraculous. In Ancient Egypt they were the tears of the god Re:

> The god Re wept and the tears
> from his eyes fell on the ground
> and turned into a bee.
> The bee made [his comb]
> and busied himself
> with the flowers of every plant;
> and so wax was made
> and also honey
> out of the tears of the god Re.
>
> (Salt papyri; British Museum)

The procreation of bees being supernatural, they, more than most animals, were believed to embody the souls of men after death. They could fly, and thus reach the gods in the heavens; they made a humming noise like the unsubstantial and ethereal winds. Moreover their dwelling on earth was a dark cavity which some scholars regard as a symbol of the womb where the human soul itself was generated. The use of honey as the first food of the newly born would help to ensure that the soul remained in the body, since bee-souls are naturally fond of honey. We may note Isaiah's prophecy (7: 14–15): 'Therefore the Lord himself shall give you a sign; behold, a virgin [young woman] shall conceive, and bear a son, and shall call his name Immanuel. Butter and honey shall he eat, that he may know to refuse the evil, and choose the good.' King Solomon's exhortation about honey is often referred to as the advice of a father to a grown man: 'My son, eat thou honey, because it is good; and the honeycomb, which is sweet to thy taste: so shall the knowledge of wisdom be unto thy soul.' (Proverbs 24: 13–14). But might it not have been addressed to a new-born son, as part of the birth rite?

The idea that honey benefits souls newly arrived in this world was later extended to bees, and many a wise philosopher, eloquent speaker and inspired poet was believed to owe his outstanding ability to the fact that bees, or a swarm of them, had alighted on his mouth in infancy. A few examples are Plato, Sophocles, Xenophon, Virgil, St. Ambrose, and St. Basil. Perhaps the origin of the idea that honey and bees could enable men to rise to god-like heights had something to do with the strength imparted by mead.

Bees, having a divine origin, could foretell the future, and were widely used in omens. Most of the evidence still extant comes from Greek, Roman and Christian times, but there is some from Africa and India. And in China, Wang Shin-Chin reported in 1691 that people living in the mountains south of Yan-yüe considered days on which bees swarmed to be lucky, and thus chose them for marriages, business transactions, and so on: 'So wonderful is the mystic instinct of these animals, which enables them to communicate freely with the Creator.'

One ability accredited very widely to bees was foreknowledge of the weather. Part of this was presumably straight observation – and one frail elderly man I knew kept bees solely so that he could tell whether the weather was suitable for him to go out (if the bees flew, yes; if not, no). A simple English rhyme that has survived is:

> If the bees stay at home,
> Rain will soon come;
> If they fly away,
> Fine will be the day.

Even the scientist Jan Swammerdam (1637–80), in his great work *Libre naturae*, had faith in the bees' foreknowledge of weather: 'Among the wonders in the real economy of bees, nothing more deserves our attention than the certain presage they have of rain.'

Rock paintings provide further evidence of the awe in which bees were held. Chapter 5 shows several early rock paintings of bees and their nests. In many such prehistoric paintings, it is found that one subject has been painted on a place previously occupied by another subject. But certain subjects were not painted over, and these are recognized as having a magico-religious significance for the people who executed the paintings. In a study of several thousand paintings in Ndedema Gorge in the Drakensberg Mountains of South Africa (where there are a good number of bee paintings), bees and allied subjects ranked third in being left free from later overpainting, being surpassed only by the eland and by mythical creatures; all other animals ranked below bees, and human figures lowest of all, i.e. they were most often painted over. Bees were usually painted as a dark body, with white wings spread out as in flight (for peripheral bees in a flying swarm, wings were sometimes omitted). The impression is very realistic, as is that of the human figures and of the animals. So to the Bushmen and others who made these paintings, bees were among the most sacred of animals, and almost certainly their honey was sacred too.

ANCIENT AND MEDIEVAL RELIGION:
BEES AS A MODEL OF THE CHRISTIAN LIFE

The belief in the sacredness of honey was carried over into early religions and, later, into the Christian church. Honey and milk were a constituent part of the communion given to neophytes, and in the Egyptian and Ethiopian churches the custom still continues, although in the Roman church it ceased in the seventh century. Saint Gregory, who was Pope from 590 to 604, wrote: 'When the grace of the Holy Spirit bathes us, it fills us with honey and butter equally. Honey falls from above, butter is drawn from the milk of animals, so honey is from the air, butter from the flesh.'

The following is a benediction of milk and honey that was used in the primitive Church as part of the baptismal communion, and also – almost without change – as a blessing for them as part of the daily food. It is taken from a tenth-century manuscript of Saint Gall:

> Bless O Lord also those of thy creatures
> that are the sources of honey and milk.
> Give thy servants to drink from the source
> of the water of eternal life
> which is the spirit of truth,
> and feed them with this milk and honey,
> as thou O Lord promised our fathers
> Abraham, Isaac and Jacob,
> to lead them to the promised land,
> a land flowing with milk and honey.
> Join therefore thy servants, O Lord,
> in the Holy Spirit,
> as honey and milk are joined,
> that we may be united
> in Jesus Christ our Lord.

One of the recensions of the Ancient Laws of Wales, probably codified from earlier material round about 950 but preserved in manuscripts written four centuries later, carries a similar refrain:

The origin of Bees is from Paradise, and on account of the sin of man they came hence, and God conferred his blessing upon them, and *therefore the mass cannot be said without the wax.*

The idea of the Christian holiness and percipience of the bee colony lived on for many centuries. In 1582 the calendar we now use was introduced by Pope Gregory, to replace the older one of Pope Julian, which had got out of phase with the seasons. There was ten days' difference between the two calendars, and much argument arose at the time as to which was correct. In the north of England, and elsewhere, there was a belief that the bees made a buzzing or humming sound in their hives at midnight on

Christmas Eve. Such was the faith of people in Yorkshire in their bees' knowledge of such things, that they listened on Christmas Eve according to *both* calendars, so that the bees could tell them which was really the anniversary of the Nativity. It is reported that the bees followed the old Julian calendar.

Thus far, honey carries with it the idea of beneficence and goodness, and bees are holy and wise. But the advent of Christianity also influenced the nature of the beliefs and customs we have been considering in a further, rather curious way. The religious focus shifted from the honey to the bees, because of their apparently ordered mode of existence and, above all, their apparent chastity – procreation notwithstanding.

Saint Ambrose, Bishop of Milan from 374 to 397, who is often regarded as the patron saint of beekeepers, wrote:

Let, then, your work be as it were a honeycomb, for virginity is fit to be compared to bees, so laborious is it, so modest, so continent. The bee feeds on dew, it knows no marriage couch, it makes honey. The virgin's dew is the divine word, for the words of God descend like the dew. The virgin's modesty is unstained nature. The virgin's produce is the fruit of the lips, without bitterness, abounding in sweetness. They work in common, and their fruit is in common.

The final argument we quoted from Aristotle still stood unchallenged: 'none of them [the bees] has ever yet been seen copulating, whereas this would have often happened if the sexes had existed in them'. In the Christian church, which set so much store by chastity as advocated by Saint Paul, the already sacred honey thus acquired even greater merit, and beeswax as a cult object acquired a new importance, which lasted into the present century. As late as 1907 the *Catholic Encyclopaedia* stated that beeswax is regarded as typifying in a most appropriate way the flesh of Jesus Christ born of a virgin mother (i.e. just as wax is born from the virgin bees). The wick of a beeswax candle symbolizes Jesus' soul, and the flame the divinity which absorbs and dominates both. The writer adds: 'This symbolism is still accepted in the Church at large.' It is interesting to compare this with an Old English text: 'Wax bitokeneth the maydenhed of Marie, Cristes modir ... Now therfor gostli bere we Crist in wombe with Marie maiden and modir' (*MS Harl.* 2276). The hymn used in the Roman church praising the Paschal candle on Holy Saturday, dating probably from the fifth century, praises the bees that provide the wax for the candle, 'who produce posterity, rejoice in offspring, yet retain their virginity'.*

The orderliness of a community of chaste bees was made use of as an example for a community of monks or nuns: the leader bee became the bishop, and the 'court' round him/her the choir. The apogee of this praise of bees as models of the virtuous Christian life, and the concept of the Church as a celestial beehive, seems to have come in the latter part of the thirteenth century. Around 1260 Thomas of Cantimpre, Canon of a Dominican Abbey in northern France, wrote his *Bonum universale de apibus*, and this was one of the first books to be printed, in 1472. In it, he argued that as there is only one king bee in the hive, so there should be only one king, one pope. As the king does not use his sting, so the bishop must be mild. The drones correspond (rather unfairly) to the lay brothers of the monastic orders. In the evening a sudden stillness falls upon the hives, and so it should in a convent. The unity among the bees provides an example for the monks, who should also be encouraged by their virgin purity. The whole work is based on real or imagined episodes in the life of bees, which are used as precepts for the conduct of life in institutions of the church.

Many other leaders of the medieval church used the same approach. For instance Bartolomaeus Anglicus, a Franciscan, noted in his *De proprietatibus rerum*, written about 1280, that young and virgin bees work better and make better honey than the old. Bees mark out and take note of those that do not work, and later on they chastise and kill them.

Towards the end of the period when the hive was a model for the church, the papal tiara was elaborated so that it looked like one of the tall wicker or straw skeps that were then in use. I am not convinced, however, that this likeness was intentional. The

* The insistence of beeswax for candles was maintained until the present century, but latterly an admixture of other waxes has received papal sanction, at percentages that vary with the importance of the use to which the candles are put. The idea that bees 'produce posterity, rejoice in offspring, yet retain their virginity' is of course incorrect. The worker bees do not (and cannot) mate, but they do not produce the offspring. The queen produces the offspring, but only after mating with a number of drones, often 7–10 in quick succession.

25. The beehive of the Roman Church, as portrayed on the title page of a 1581 edition of *De roomsche byen-korf* by Filips van Marnix.

tiara is certainly made into a hive on the title page of *De roomsche byen-korf* [The Roman beehive], a satire by Filips van Marnix, Lord of St. Aldegonde, published in Dutch in 1569 (fig. 25). From this hive, the Pope – as the king bee – surveys the other bees, who with shorn heads, mitres and cardinals' hats are flying round him, hearing confessions, burying the dead and saying Mass. The English edition (1579) included an outspoken preface by John Still:

> Good Christian Reader, thinke it not lost labour to reade this little booke, which as it beareth the name of a Bee-Hive, so it containeth good store of wholesome hony ... Gentle Reader, thou hast such a book as will make thee privie to all the practices of the Babylonicall Beast (Rome, I mean), the denne of Dragons and Devils, which if it were translated into other tongues by the industrie of the learned, it would increase choler abundantly in the Pope, the College of Cardinalls, Monasteries of Monkes, Fraternities of Friary, Nests of Nonnes and the rest of the Pharisaical Frie ...

The identification of an organized human society with a colony of bees was by no means confined to the medieval Christian church: it has occurred in most societies where honeybees were known. The large leader bee was the Pope, Caesar, Tsar, King – later Queen – or whatever was required, and from Roman times onwards duties were allocated to different groups of bees. The drones were the only non-cooperators, and to them capital punishment was meted out to provide a salutary lesson for human malingerers or dissidents. Here is an example from Virgil's description of the building of Carthage in the *Aeneid*:

In the early summer ... the honey bees are at work, when they lead forth the full-grown young of their race, or when they pack the liquid honey and fill their combs full of sweet nectar, or receive the burdens of those that come in, or form a martial line and drive forth from the hives the drones, a lazy tribe ... even so work the Carthaginians.

I, 494–501, trans. Lonsdale & Lee

Virgil's Fourth Book of *Georgics* includes an expanded passage about the division of labour in the hive:

For some preside
O'er getting of the food, and duty-bound
Are busy in the fields; others indoors
Fix tears of daffodils and tough bark-glue
For bases to the combs, then hang thereto
The sticky wax; and some escort abroad
The grown-up sons, the city's hope and crown;
And others pack the honeyed excellence
Close, with pure nectar plumping every cell;
And some by lot are warders of the gate,
And scan the clouds in turn and watch for showers,
Or else relieve home-comers of their load,
Or all unite and chase the lazy drones
Across the border

lines 189–202, trans. T. F. Royde

Mum and the sothsegger, a rather little-known poem written in the West Midlands of England in the fourteenth century, also makes non-religious comparisons. The poet is searching for a teller of truth (*sothsegger*), but his enquiries meet no response but silence (*mum*) until, having exhausted the resources of the church, university, and other institutions, he finds an old beekeeper who is able to give a description of life in the hive that at last shows the poet how society should be ruled. Drones come in for a great slanging, for 'they devour what is due to others', but retribution comes when the bees 'kill the drones quickly and repay all their wickednesses'. The bees themselves have only good traits: 'Their works are truly wonderful ... [their king] rules them by reason and righteous judgement, through the consent of the people, who

26. Engraving that faces the opening page of *The Fourth Book of the Georgics* in the copy of Dryden's translation in the IBRA Library (1697).

'First, for thy Bees a quiet Station find', protected from the wind, and from grazing animals, and 'With Osier Floats the standing Water strow;/Of massy Stones make Bridges, if it flow.'

combine all together.' And so on.

Chaucer, in *The parson's tale*, refers, like many of the other authors, to the fact that the king bee does not sting (the King of England at that time was Richard II):

And therefore thise flyes that men clepeth [call] bees, whan they maken hir [their] king, they chesen oon that hath no prikke wherwith he may stinge.

Chaucer, however, introduces an altogether lighter note, in his use of the word *honey* as a term of endearment. In *The miller's tale* the carpenter's beloved is 'Alisoun, his hony dere' or even 'hony-comb', which is hardly used today in the same way:

> What do ye, hony-comb, sweete Alisoun
> My fair bryd, my sweete cynamome?

In the sixteenth century, passages on the same theme were written by a French author in *Fleur de vertu*, by John Lyly in *Euphues and his England*, by Michel de Montaigne in his *Essais*, and by others. A passage outstanding in every way was written in 1599 by Shakespeare, in *King Henry V* (I, ii). Like his forerunners, Shakespeare still did not know that the 'king' in the hive was a female, although Luis Méndez de Torres in Spain had in fact established this in 1586.

> Therefore doth heaven divide
> The state of man in divers functions,
> Setting endeavour in continual motion;
> To which is fixed, as an aim or butt,
> Obedience: for so work the honey-bees,
> Creatures that by a rule in nature teach
> The act of order to a peopled kingdom.
> They have a king, and officers of sorts:
> Where some, like magistrates, correct at home;
> Others, like merchants, venture trade abroad;
> Others, like soldiers, armed in their stings,
> Make boot upon the summer's velvet buds;
> Which pillage they with merry march bring home
> To the tent-royal of their emperor:
> Who, busied in his majesty, surveys
> The singing masons building roofs of gold;
> The civil citizens kneading up the honey,
> The poor mechanic porters crowding in
> Their heavy burdens at his narrow gate,
> The sad-ey'd justice, with his surly hum,
> Delivering o'er to executors pale
> The lazy yawning drone. I this infer,
> That many things, having full reference
> To one consent, may work contrariously:
> As many arrows, loosed several ways,
> Fly to one mark;
> ...
> So may a thousand actions, once afoot,
> End in one purpose, ...

SECULARIZATION FROM THE CHURCH TO THE FAMILY: TELLING THE BEES

For whatever reasons, the Christian church's adoption of the hive and its products lost some of its fervour from the sixteenth century onwards, although vestiges have remained to the present day. As a result of the Reformation, and the suppression of the monasteries in Britain in the 1530s, less wax was required for candles. Possibly the hives of bees from monasteries were distributed among various people, or at any rate swarms may have been left uncollected, available to anyone who wanted them. Also sugar was becoming less expensive; it still cost several times as much as honey, but there had been a marked drop in the difference between their prices.

One result of this 'secularization' of bees seems to have been an increase in the regard for them in a family setting, and indeed as part of the family, although still with marked Christian undertones. This is exemplified by the rite of 'telling the bees' of a death or other family event, which is one of the most widely remembered of all customs to do with bees and honey. It is often assumed that this tradition, like so many others, is a survival of primitive pre-Christian practices, but Dr. A. E. Fife made an extensive search in the principal sources of the bee lore of primitive, medieval and renaissance Europe, and could find no evidence for this. The earliest specific instance he found of any special attention being paid to bees after a death was the following passage, in a book of historical meditations by the German classical scholar Joachim Gamerarius (1500–74) translated into English in 1621 by John Molle:

Who would believe without superstition (if experience did not make it credible) that most commonly all the bees die in their hives, if the master or mistress of the house chance to die, except the hives be presently removed into some other place? And yet I know this hath happened to folks no way stained with superstition.

The next reference traced was a recommendation in J. Coler's *Oeconomia* (Mainz, 1645) that bees of a deceased person should not be purchased, because they would also shortly die. Much later there was a statement that in seventeenth-century France hives were placed in mourning, with black crêpe, at the death of the master, for it was believed that the bees would otherwise die or abscond. Then on 13 September 1790 the *Argus* reported an incident in Devon: a servant girl was told to turn the hives around on their stands as the corpse of the deceased master was being carried from the house. Instead, however, the hives were turned over on their sides, with the result that the members of the funeral train were badly stung.

The first half of the nineteenth century was the heyday of the practice of 'telling the bees', and this declined thereafter until, by say 1950, in many places a living example became rare enough to make news.

What was in fact told to the bees, and what was the ritual for doing it? The basic principle underlying the practice seems to have been the recognition that the family's bee colonies were members of the household. News of the death of the head of a household was universally passed on, and the deaths of other members of it were sometimes similarly marked.

In about half of the 700 records obtained by Dr. Fife, no more was done than *telling* the bees (according to a prescribed rite, which varied from place to place). This applied in Slav countries, and often in German-speaking areas, although there the commonest rite was to move the hives to a different position (as Gamerarius reported) or so that they faced in a different direction (as the Devonshire girl had been told to do). In Germany a few people also put their hives into mourning, and in France this action was even more common than telling the bees of the death; black crêpe, or a bow of black ribbon was *de rigueur*. In about half of the 284 cases recorded in Britain and North America, to which the custom also spread, nothing more was done than telling the bees. A quarter also put the hives in mourning, and a few moved the hives or presented some of the funeral food to the bees, a custom which seems to have been absent in continental Europe.

With regard to the actual telling, usually each hive had to be approached and notified after rapping three times, possibly with the key of the house. Sometimes the news must be whispered; sometimes the bees must also be consoled and comforted, or even invited to the funeral. The words might be something like this.

> The master is dead
>
> The master's dead but don't you go,
> Your mistress will be a good mistress to you.
>
> Bees, Bees, Awake!
> Your master is dead
> And another you must take.
>
> You are invited to the funeral of A— B—, at such and such
> a time and place.

The person carrying out the rite must be variously the heir or another member of the immediate family, or a relative, or a faithful servant. The bees were to be treated as respected members of the family.

From the evidence available, it seems clear that the original, primary custom referred only to the death of the master, and its application extended thence to the mistress and sometimes also to other members of the family. Similarly, especially in Germanic areas, the custom sometimes spread from telling the bees to telling other animals around the house (cows, dogs, birds, etc.), and even trees, crops and other plants, and some inanimate objects. But available evidence makes it clear that the bees were the *primary* recipients of family news.

Records of telling the bees of a death are about eight times as numerous as records of telling them of a happy family event that was also marked by a church ceremony: marriage, birth and baptism. In about half these cases the hives would be provided with some visible sign of rejoicing – a red cloth or some other wedding favour, or food from the banquet.

The usual penalty expected if the respective rituals were not carried out correctly was that the bees would dwindle and die, or alternatively fly away, or fail to produce honey. This, and other more scattered pieces of evidence, all suggest that bees were a primary sharer in the family's joys and sorrows, and indeed in its spiritual life; they held a unique mystic and spiritual importance in the life of the household. It is noteworthy that in the German language, where words for some actions differ according to whether they are applied to men or animals, the word used for bees is the one used for human beings. Thus to eat is *essen* not *fressen*, and to die is *sterben* not *verenden*.

The custom of telling the bees has been substantiated in the whole of continental Europe except the south-west – Portugal, Spain and the Balearic Islands; Corsica and Sardinia; Sicily and Italy. Fife sums up by saying that 'it is limited exclusively to Christian territory, belonging to what may be called a Celto-Germanic-Slavic belt which is for the most part beyond the 45th degree north latitude'.

BEES PROVIDE A CONVENIENT POLITICAL IMAGE

Well outside the intimacy of family life lies the harsh and bitter world of politics. This in some measure inherited the earlier concept of the bee colony as a model of a religious or secular society, but the moral tone became changed over the years, and varied according to the parallels that any particular writer wished to draw.

The Parliament of bees, a satire by John Daye, was written possibly as early as 1607 but was not published until 1641. Its subtitle was: 'A Beehive furnisht with twelve Honeycombes as Pleasant as Profitable, being an Allegoricall Description of the Actions of Good and Bad Men in these our daies.' The leader of the hive was Mr. Bee, who acted as Pro-Rex in the Parliament under Oberon.

In 1660 James Howell published the *Parley of beasts*: 'Know, sir, that we also have a religion as well as so exact a government among us here; our hummings you speak of are so many hymns to the Great God of Nature.' Howell wrote of sick bees ('for all that live must die'), and John Gay's *Fables*, the first of which were published in 1727, include one on 'Degenerate bees'. A better-known work, by his contemporary Bernard de Mandeville, was published in 1714 as *The Fable of the Bees: or, Private Vices, Publick Benefits*, but it had already appeared anonymously (in 1705) as *The Grumbling Hive: or Knaves turn'd Honest*. Mandeville republished it, and the final 1724 book had many additions and commentaries. His main argument was that the capitalist economy emerging at the time depended for its prosperity on the vices and 'most hateful qualities' of its citizens. Not surprisingly, the satire initiated a flood of denunciations and attacks. The complete book was republished in 1970 by Penguin Books, so those who wish to study it can do so. The quotations below will be enough to suggest to some readers that the *Fable* is no more outmoded now than the beehive on which its concept is based.

> A spacious Hive well stock'd with Bees,
> That lived in Luxury and Ease;
> And yet as fam'd for Laws and Arms,
> As yielding large and early Swarms;
> Was counted the great Nursery
> Of Sciences and Industry.
> No Bees had better Government,
> More Fickleness, or less Content.
> They were not Slaves to Tyranny,
> Nor ruled by wild Democracy;
> . . . . . .
>
> Vast Numbers thronged the fruitful Hive;
> Yet those vast Numbers made 'em thrive;
> Millions endeavouring to supply
> Each other's Lust and Vanity;
> Whilst other Millions were employ'd.
> To see their Handy-work destroy'd;
> . . . . . .
>
> The Soldiers, that were forced to fight,
> If they survived, got Honour by't;
> . . . . . .
>
> Till quite disabled, and put by,
> They lived on half their Salary;
> Whilst others never came in Play,
> And staid at Home for Double Pay.
> . . . . . .
>
> For there was not a Bee, but would
> Get more, I won't say, than he should;

At the end, 'few in the vast Hive remain'; but, satisfactorily,

> Hard'ned with Toils, and Exercise
> They counted Ease it self a Vice;
> Which so improved their Temperance;
> That, to avoid Extravagance,
> They flew into a hollow Tree,
> Blest with Content and Honesty.

In contrast to these political fables and satires, other authors used the model of the bee colony to express their loyalty to their sovereign, or (as in Samuel Hartlib's book, published during the Protectorate) to a commonwealth form of government. Hartlib used the title *The reformed commonwealth of bees*, and – in 1655, without a king as head of state – he could openly praise the queen bee as a female:

This is a feminine Monarchie, the females governe ... But see this royall Queen of Bees, how qualified; she is faire, comely, loving, harmlesse, gentle, peaceable, yea a vigilant Queen, a royall emblem of governement. See also the cares, labour, diligence, providence and provision, watchfulness, valour and loyalty of this commonwealth. How would that commonwealth flourish, where the members joyning in such unanimity, should all (setting aside private gaine) aime wholly at the public weale: and in defence thereof esteem nothing too deare to bestow, no not their lives?

After the monarchy was restored in 1660, John Evelyn got Moses Rusden appointed as the King's Bee Master, and Rusden's book, *A further discovery of bees* (1679), reflected the political change:

Since therefore Nature will herein be made appear to be the Favourer and Founder of Monarchy; and that such ingenious, laborious and profitable Creatures do voluntarily and constantly betake themselves to that Governement, I do most humbly beseech your Majesties gracious Patronage and Protection, whilest I demonstrate and vindicate this Truth, by the perpetual practice of the Bees: ... I make it my prayer that all your Majesties Subjects may be as loyal to your Majesty, as conformable to your laws, and as beneficial to the Publick, as these little People are to their Soveraign, to their customs and their republick, in which they most examplarily labour and obey.

There were many variations on the theme as the years passed by. For instance at the height of Queen Victoria's reign the *Illustrated London News* described the 1851 Exhibition in the Crystal Palace as 'The Great Gathering of the Industrious Bees':

How beautifully is the great Palace of Industry represented by Milton's *Mansion of Industry* ... where more than two hundred thousand little labourers are diligently engaged in their various daily duties, while their reigning sovereign reposes quietly in her regal apartment, attended to by her subjects with the utmost regard to her comfort and convenience.

BEES IN THE MINDS OF MEN TODAY

What place do bees have in the minds of men today? Many of the ideas we have encountered in unrolling the tapestry of past beliefs and sentiments about bees are still retained somewhere in the world.

Kilvert's Diary for Ascension Day in 1870 reads:

The bells ringing for the Ascension. Went to Church with my Father through the sunny golden fields variegated with clover and daisies and ground ivy. The Church bell tolling for service through the elms. A small congregation, but many bees buzzing about the Church windows as if a swarm were flying. My father says this has happened on several Ascension days and once the Churchwarden John Bryant came after a swarm of his to the Church on Ascension day, clinking a frying pan and shovel. My father told him that the bees showed the people the way to Church.

The Christian belief in the sanctity of bees and their products, and the invocation of God on their behalf, are by no means a thing of the past. In 1976 a visitor to the mountains of eastern Tyrol found that many of the beehouses had a *Bienensegen* (bee-blessing) displayed on the wall; a typical example may be translated as follows:

> Almighty Lord and God –
> Thou hast created heaven and earth,
> and all animals for the benefit of mankind.
> Thou hast charged the servants of Thy Holy Church
> with the making of candles from bees' wax
> and with the lighting of them
> for celebrating Thy Holy Mystery in the Church.
> May Thy blessing be upon this beehouse
> and upon the bees in it,
> that they may multiply and bring a harvest,
> and be protected from all harm,
> so that their produce may be used
> for Thine honour and glory.
> Through Christ our Lord, Amen.

Below is a translation of words on an embroidered banner carried in procession to a 1976 harvest festival in Germany:

> Our Saviour and Redeemer –
> Take into Thy care the bees
> That give wax for the altar,
> Nourish our bodies,
> And teach us industry and order –
> God's blessing be on them.

The honeybee colony is still used as a model for the state, whether this is a kingdom or a republic – it needs only a change of name from *queen* to *mother* (*matka* in Russian). The following passage shows how the colony is described in terms of a sheikhdom. It was published in 1977, in an article describing how honey is harvested from small single-comb nests of *Apis florea* by people in the Sultanate of Oman in the extreme east of the Arabian peninsula.

In rural Oman ... the social structure and division of labour of a honey-bee colony are pictured in terms of traditional tribal structure. The queen is the (male) *shaykh*, and the workers are the people (*sh'ab*); the drones, being black, are called slaves (*khadim*). The slaves are said to bring water to the colony, carried in their stomachs, while the people bring 'honey' and pollen from the flowers – the former carried in their stomachs and the latter on their legs. Accepting a tribal structure, it is naturally assumed that the people and the slaves look after their own reproduction, and that the *shaykh* has a wife who produces the *shaykh*'s sons – after the winter and after the summer. It is observed that, when a young *shaykh* is in the colony, rivalling his father, swarming occurs, and it is presumed to arise from a division of loyalties amongst the *sh'ab*. Omani beekeepers therefore watch for queen cells and destroy either the cells or the larvae.

The above examples are direct survivals from similar beliefs held many centuries ago. Over and above such beliefs, we inherit the traditions of our forebears in indirect and less obvious ways. To such traditions each generation adds new concepts and ideas, but these too are affected by the culture in which their initiators are reared. In Europe, where honey and wax have been harvested from bees for thousands of years, bees are still regarded with approbation in many countries. I constantly notice how widely a bee motif is used in advertising to represent thrift, foresight or productivity, and a series of hexagonal cells is chosen as a background pattern to a display or emblem. This would not be done if bees were associated in people's minds with stings rather than with honey – sweetness – goodness; and to some this sequence is still extended to magic and sacredness.

In a recent analysis of one hundred newspaper items on bees and beekeeping in England, almost all were favourable or neutral: over half were straight reports about swarms, beekeepers' meetings, imports of queens, etc.; a quarter described the natural history of bees, and the need to protect them from poisonous chemicals. There were six items reporting (the same) theft of two hives, and two on stinging. This would not be the state of affairs in all countries, but in much of Europe bees are protected by the very long tradition of beekeeping. Socialist countries are also supported by Lenin's benevolence towards beekeeping. In April 1919 he signed a *Decree for the protection of beekeeping* for the Sovnarkom RSFSR, as its President; the translation (by Renata Castle and John Pierson) runs as follows:

1. When the labour of individuals or members of their families is used for beekeeping, it is forbidden to limit by any rules either the number of apiaries or the number of hives. Such apiaries cannot be requisitioned or brought under any departments, but must be left in the possession of the beekeepers themselves, and therefore any claims by any organizations or persons to take over for their own use already existing working apiaries are unlawful.
2. Whatever decrees there may be limiting the quantity of honey which is to be set aside for the feeding of bees or for personal consumption are to be disregarded.
3. Taxation of beekeepers shall take place under the general direction of the finances and expenses of local councils. Beekeepers do not come under special tax laws.
4. Agricultural departments are bound to show every co-operation to all organizations and persons desiring to occupy themselves with beekeeping, and to offer every possibility to establish apiaries in the most convenient places. When an apiarist is transferred and new plots of land allocated, or when hives and equipment are moved to such new places, there must not be any limitation of beekeeping.
N.B. All working beekeepers have the right to demand from the veterinary workers' commission certificates of safe conduct and technical help.
5. Limitation of the exchange or sale of bees from apiaries is forbidden.
6. All orders and decrees of local authorities contrary to the present decree must be changed.
7. Those violating this decree will be prosecuted.

In accordance with the laws of R.S.F.S.R.

(signed) V. Ul'yanov (Lenin)

In Britain during the Second World War, Sir Winston Churchill was concerned for the nation's bees:

Prime Minister to Minister of Agriculture and Minister of Food, 19th April 1943
   I understand you have discontinued the small sugar ration which was allowed to bees, and which in the spring months is most important to their work throughout the whole year.

Pray let me know what was the amount previously allotted. What is the amount of sugar still issued to professional beekeepers, and what is the saving in starving the bees of private owners?

The Second World War, Vol. 4, App. C (p. 849)

The care and attention devoted to bees is certainly not world-wide. In many countries without sufficient knowledge – and in some countries with it – foraging bees, and even whole colonies and whole apiaries, are killed by the improper use of insecticides on the very crops the bees should be pollinating. The spread of 'Africanized' bees in South America has provided much drama for the sensational press, because these bees are extremely efficient at defending their nests. It has also provided higher honey harvests for some of the beekeepers in Latin America, because the bees are also efficient at foraging and storing honey.

The age-old belief that bees are connected with fertility has been given substance by the discovery that they play an important part in pollinating fruit and seed crops. This discovery is only two or three centuries old. In an important paper in 1750, Arthur Dobbs stated that pollen is the 'male seed' which fertilizes the ovum, and described the constancy of each foraging bee to a single kind of flower:

Upon whatsoever Flower I saw it first alight and gather the *Farina*, it continued gathering from that Kind of Flower. ... So that if it began to load from a Daisy, it continued loading from them, neglecting Clover, Honeysuckle, Violets, &c. ... Now if the Facts are so, and my Observations true, I think that Providence has appointed the Bee to be very instrumental in promoting the increase of Vegetables. ...

The conservationists among us may well see a colony of bees as an archetypal user of food resources in a way that conserves them – and indeed, through pollination, increases them. The following verse was written by George Herbert in an age more totally anthropocentric than ours, in 1633, long before the process of pollination was understood, but it may serve as an endpiece to this book:

Bees work for man; and yet they never bruise
Their master's flower, but leave it, having done,
As fair as ever, and as fit to use:
So both the flower doth stay, and honey run.

Appendix 1

PRODUCING YOUR OWN HONEY

If you do not keep bees but are tempted to do so, it is best to start soon after the active growing season has got going. In temperate zones this is the spring; in the tropics it may be the onset of winter, or the beginning or end of the rains. You can then start with a small colony known as a 'nucleus', which is easy to inspect; you have the bees' most active season in front of you, which can provide a graduated series of opportunities to learn about your bees; and your mistakes need not bring disaster in their train. If you start with a larger colony late in the season, your preliminary mistakes may leave it unable to survive until the next active season; if you start late with a small colony, it will not be large enough to survive. In any case, your first year should be used for learning, not for intensive honey production.

As soon as you become interested in the idea, start making the following enquiries:

1. Check that you will have somewhere to put several hives of bees (not just one) where they will not be a nuisance to other people or to animals etc.; see also 3 below.

2. Check that no one living with you or close by is known to have a history of hypersensitivity (allergy) to bees or bee stings.

3. From a public library or information department, find out what national or regional legislation is in force that relates to beekeeping. In some countries all beekeepers, or all those with more than a certain number of hives, must register them; in others it is forbidden to keep hives within a certain distance of a public highway, or in large towns, or even in any built-up area. There may be customs or regulations on the siting of hives in relation to hives of other beekeepers.

4. If you are clear on the three points above, get in touch with your national, regional or local Department of Agriculture, to find the name and address of your local beekeeping or apiculture officer. He may be attached to any one of several Divisions, for instance Horticulture, Veterinary Medicine, Plant Protection, or Entomology; he may work only part-time in apiculture. Provided such an officer exists, it is likely to be part of his duty to advise any beekeeper who asks for such help. Even if his constituency is in theory limited to large-scale beekeepers, he is unlikely to refuse a request from a new beekeeper who is eager to learn how to start on the right lines. He may well become a valued friend.

5. From your contacts in 3 or 4, get the addresses of both your national beekeepers' association and the nearest local association. The former may have information leaflets – about beekeeping methods, nectar and pollen plants, hives in use, insurance of hives, and third-party insurance for any possible damage by bees – which may be provided free with an association subscription. The local association is a likely source of practical help and encouragement, and it may run a programme of lectures, films and practical demonstrations. Swarms or colonies of bees, and beekeeping equipment, may also be obtainable. Unlike beekeeping officers financed from public funds – to which the public contributes, directly or indirectly – a beekeepers' association is organized by its members, often on a very small budget, and all or most officers provide their services voluntarily. So join up, and pay your subscription, *before* you start asking for the help you will need, which will then be gladly and generously given.

6. Look for opportunities to see beekeeping films, through the association, on TV, or in any other way. You can see on film many events that you may never see in real life, because bees are so small and move so quickly: a queen mating, a larva hatching from an egg, two queens fighting, and so on. You can also see beekeeping operations being carried out, and how other bee-keepers manage their bees.

7. From the beekeeping contacts you have established, or from a public library, ask for details of beekeeping magazines. There is likely to be one published under the auspices of your national beekeepers' association. Also, since beekeepers are inveterate

individualists, there may well be one or more 'independent' journals. There may also be a local newsletter. Write to ask for a specimen copy of each, so that you can decide which appeals to you most. The various advertisements will acquaint you with the location of firms that sell hives, etc. These firms will gladly send you their catalogues, which usually range from beginner's outfits to the honey containers and labels that you will need later on.

8. If at all possible, arrange to visit one of your new-found beekeeping acquaintances when he or she is opening a hive for inspection and possible manipulation. Most beekeepers enjoy showing an interested novice the various features of a colony of bees; they will also explain what they and you can do to minimize the chance of being stung. Some beekeeper-demonstrators may offer a multitude of instructions on points of detail, and it will not necessarily be easy for you to distinguish between those that are of primary importance (for example, take care not to damage the queen), those that represent good beekeeping practice (for example, collect discarded pieces of wax and comb and take them away from the apiary with you), and those that are the preference or custom of the individual beekeeper (for example, always/never wear gloves when handling bees). You will sort such things out gradually when you have your own bees.

9. The following are some of the questions you may want to put to a knowledgeable beekeeper in your locality before you get bees of your own:

(a) How much honey do beekeepers reckon to get in the area, in a good year and in a poor year?

(b) When are the flows which give the surplus honey, and when is the swarming period?

(c) Where are you likely to be able to get *gentle* bees? (While you are learning how to handle bees, and perhaps afterwards, it is more important for your bees to be easy to handle than highly productive.)

(d) Where is the best place for you to site your hive(s)?

(e) What is the standard hive where you live? If there is no one standard, what type of hive is used by most people? Whether you buy new or second-hand hives and fittings, do not acquire non-standard material, because you will not be able to use it in conjunction with what you acquire later.

(f) Is there any local scheme for hiring honey-extracting equipment, so that you need not buy it?

10. Borrow from your local library some of the books listed in *Further Reading*, read them, and buy one or two that you get on best with. Writers of beekeeping manuals differ very much in their approach, and it is important that the books you come to use are not only sound and sensible, but are the sort that you can work with.

11. When you open a hive, always wear a bee-tight veil, which leaves no gap through which a bee can enter; if you are wearing trousers, tie them close at the bottom. Do not let anyone else come near the hive who is not similarly protected. To start with, wear bee-tight gloves (or cuffs only) when you handle frames of bees. Use a smoker, and have a hive-tool available to loosen hive parts that the bees have stuck together. These precautions may or may not be necessary on a specific occasion. But if you do not take them, especially while you are inexperienced in handling bees, someone's bravado could result in a sting on the face, which can be unpleasant, or even in the eye, which can be serious. Moreover, it will give you confidence to *know* that the bees cannot get at your face, hair or hands.

People become enthusiastic about keeping bees for various reasons and at various seasons. In summer they hear talk of beekeeping; at the end of it they see fresh honey for sale; and in winter they may see films or hear radio programmes or lectures about bees. The time between deciding to keep bees and being able to start often seems frustratingly long, but it can be a most valuable period, during which knowledge is gained that ensures later success and enables the new beekeeper to save money by making a wise initial capital outlay. Alternatively, detailed consideration may show the enthusiast that for some reason beekeeping is not practicable for him or her in the immediate future.

Appendix 2

Table 1. Plants that are important sources of the world's honey

The 232 plants are listed in alphabetical order of their botanical families, a common name being added where one exists. Entries in the five columns on the right indicate the presence of the plant as a honey source in the different continents:

N, S   north, south temperate zones ⎫ brackets indicate presence,
T   tropics/subtropics   ⎭ but not as a honey source.

The extent of the continents is:

Old World	Europe	N		
	Asia	N	T	
	Africa	N	T	S
New World	America	N	T	S
	Oceania		T	S

	Europe	Asia	Africa	America	Oceania
Acanthaceae					
Carvia callosa Bremk.		T			
Dyschoriste Nees spp.			T		
Hypoestes Soland. spp.			T	(S)	
Isoglossa Oerst. spp.			T		
Lepedagathis cuspidata Nees		T			
Monechma Hochst.			T		
Thelepaepale ixiocephala Bremk.		T			
Aceraceae					
Acer L. spp. MAPLE, etc.	N	N	N	NS	(S)
A. pseudoplatanus L. SYCAMORE	N	N		(S)	
Amaryllidaceae					
Agave L. spp. AGAVE		T	TS	T(S)	
A. sisalana Perrine SISAL		T	T	T(S)	
Anacardiaceae					
Anacardium occidentale L. CASHEW NUT		T	T	T(S)	
Lannea A. Rich. spp.		T	T		
Mangifera indica L. MANGO		T	T	T(S)	
Pistacia vera L. ⟨PISTACHIO		T	T	T(S)	
Rhus L. spp. SUMAC, etc.	N	NTS	NTS	NT(S)	T

	Europe	Asia	Africa	America	Oceania
Aquifoliaceae					
Ilex L. spp. HOLLY, etc.	N	NTS	NTS	NT(S)	(S)
Ilex glabra Gray GALLBERRY				N	
Asclepiadaceae					
Asclepias L. spp. MILKWEED, SILKWEED			NS	N(S)	
Asclepias syriaca L.			(S)	N	
Balsaminaceae					
Impatiens Riv. ex L. spp. BALSAM	N	T	T	N(S)	
Impatiens glandulifera Royle	N	T	T	N(S)	
Berberidaceae					
Berberis L. spp. BARBERRY	N	N	N	N(S)	S
Bombacaceae					
*Ceiba pentandra Gaertn. SILK-COTTON TREE		T			
Durio zibethinus Murr. DURYON		T			
Boraginaceae					
Borago officinalis L. BORAGE	N	N	N	NTS	S
Echium lycopsis L. PURPLE VIPER'S BUGLOSS	N	N	N	N	S
Echium vulgare L. VIPER'S BUGLOSS, BLUEWEED	N	N	N	NS	S
Cactaceae					
Opuntia Miller (200 spp.) PRICKLY PEAR, etc.	N		N	NT(S)	S
Combretaceae					
Combretum L. spp.			T	T	
*Terminalia L. spp.		T			
Compositae					
Arctotheca calendula (L.) H. Levyns CAPE WEED			S		S
Aster L. spp. ASTER	N	NT		N	
*Baccharis L.				T	
Bidens L. spp. SPANISH NEEDLE, etc.		NTS	T(S)	NT(S)	
*Calea pinnatifida Lese				T	
Calea urticifolia (Miller) DC. JALACATE (Spanish)				T	
Carduus (Tourn.) L. spp. THISTLES	N	N	T	(S)	(S)
Carthamus tinctorius L. SAFFLOWER	N	N		N(S)	
Centaurea L. (600 spp.) KNAPWEED, CORNFLOWER, etc.	N	N		N	S
Cirsium Miller spp. THISTLES	N	N	T		S
Cynara cardunculus L. CARDOON	N			S	
*Eupatorium L. spp.			T		
Guizotia abyssinica Cass. NIGER		T	T	(S)	
Helianthus annuus L. SUNFLOWER	N	N	NTS	NTS	(S)
Senecio jacobaea L. and spp. RAGWORT	N	N	S	NTS	S

	Europe	Asia	Africa	America	Oceania
Solidago L. spp. GOLDEN ROD	N	NTS		N(S)	
Taraxacum officinale Weber DANDELION	N	N	NS	NTS	S
Vernonia Schreb. spp. IRONWEED		T	T	T(S)	
Viguiera grammatoglossa DC. ACAHUAL				T	
Viguiera helianthoides H.B.K. ROMERILLO (Spanish), TAH (Maya)				T	
Convolvulaceae					
Ipomoea L. spp. CAMPANILLA, BELL-FLOWER,			(T)		
MORNING GLORY, AGUINALDO (Spanish)			T	NT(S)	T
Rivea corymbosa (L.) Hall AGUINALDO BLANCO (Spanish)		T		T(S)	
Cruciferae					
Brassica juncea (L.) Czern. INDIAN MUSTARD, CHINESE MUSTARD		T		T(S)	
Brassica napus L. subsp. *oleifera* DC. SUMMER/WINTER/SWEDE RAPE	N	N		NS	S
Brassica rapa (*B. campestris* L.) var. *oleifera* (WINTER) RAPE – TURNIP RAPE	N	N		NT(S)	S
Brassica rapa (*B. campestris* L.) var. *sarson* SARSON		T		(S)	
Brassica rapa L. (*B. campestris* L.) var. *toria* TORIA		T		(S)	
Sinapis alba L., *Brassica nigra* (L.) Koch WHITE, BLACK MUSTARD	N	N		NT(S)	
Sinapis arvensis L. CHARLOCK, WILD MUSTARD	N	N		N	S
Cucurbitaceae					
Cucumis L. spp. CUCUMBER, MELON, etc.	N	NTS	NTS	NTS	T(S)
Cunoniaceae					
Weinmannia racemosa L. KAMAHI					S
Weinmannia silvicola Soland ex A. Cunn. TOWAI, TAWHERO					S
Cyrillaceae					
Cyrilla racemiflora L., *Cliftonia ligustrina* TI-TI				NT	
Ebenaceae					
Diospyros virginiana L. and spp. PERSIMMON, etc.		NT	S	NT(S)	
Ericaceae					
Calluna vulgaris (L.) Hull LING HEATHER	N			N	S
Erica L. spp. HEATHS	N		(T)S	(S)	S
Erica cinerea L. BELL HEATHER	N				
Oxydendrum arboreum DC. SOURWOOD				N	
Rhododendron ferrugineum L., *R. hirsutum* L. ALPINE ROSE	N				

	Europe	*Asia*	*Africa*	*America*	*Oceania*
Rhododendron ponticum L. RHODODENDRON	N	N		(S)	
Vaccinium L. spp. BLUEBERRY, HUCKLEBERRY,					
CRANBERRY, WHORTLEBERRY, BILBERRY, etc.	N	N	(T)	N	
Eucryphiaceae					
Eucryphia Cav. spp. LEATHERWOOD					S
Euphorbiaceae					
Croton L. (600 spp.) CROTON		T	T	NT(S)	
*Hevea brasiliensis Muell. Arg. RUBBER TREE		T		(T)	
Ricinus communis L. CASTOR-OIL PLANT		T	T	T(S)	
Fagaceae					
Castanea sativa Miller SWEET CHESTNUT	N	N		S	
Quercus L. spp. OAK	N	NT		N(S)	
Hippocastanaceae					
Aesculus L. spp. HORSE CHESTNUT	N	N		N(S)	
Hydrophyllaceae					
Phacelia Juss. (*tanacetifolia* Bentham and spp.)					
PHACELIA	N	N		N(S)	
Labiatae					
Dracocephalum moldavicum L. MOLDAVIAN BALM	N	N		(S)	
Lavandula spica L. LAVENDER	N		N	S	
Lavandula stoechas L. FRENCH LAVENDER	N		N		(S)
Mentha L. spp. MINT	N	N	N	NS	S
Nepeta L. spp. CATMINT, etc.	N	N	NT	N(S)	(S)
Ocimum L. spp.		T	T	T(S)	TS
Origanum L. *vulgare* MARJORAM	N	NT		NT(S)	
*Plectranthus mollis Spreng.		N			
Rosmarinus officinalis L. ROSEMARY	N		N	(S)	
Salvia L. (550 spp.) SAGE, etc.	N	N	NT	NTS	S
Satureia L. spp. SAVORY	N		N	N(S)	
Stachys annua (L.) L. WOUNDWORT	N	N		(S)	
Teucrium scorodonia L. WOODSAGE	N			N(S)	
Thymus L. (150 spp.) THYME	N	N	N	N(S)	S
Lauraceae					
*Actinodaphne angustifolia Nees		T			
*Alseodaphne semecarpaefolia Nees		T			
Persea americana Miller AVOCADO		NT	S	NT(S)	
Leguminosae					
Acacia L. spp. WATTLE, etc.		NTS	NTS	NTS	TS
*Albizia Durazz.			T		
Arachis (*hypogaea* L. and spp.) GROUND NUT,					
PEANUT, EARTH NUT			T	T(S)	
Astragalus L. spp. MILK VETCH	N	N	N	(S)	

	Europe	Asia	Africa	America	Oceania
Brachystegia Bentham spp.			T		
Caragana arborescens Lam. (SIBERIAN) PEA TREE		N		N(S)	
Dalbergia L. spp. ROSEWOOD, SISSOO, etc.		T	T	T(S)	
Erythrina L. spp. CORAL TREE		T			T
Gleditsia L. spp. HONEY LOCUST		NT	TS	NT(S)	
Glycine max (L.) Merr. SOYA-BEAN		N		NS	
Haematoxylon campechianum L. LOGWOOD, CAMPECHE			T	T(S)	
Hedysarum coronarium L. SULLA	N			NS	
Julbernardia globiflora (Bentham) Troupin, *paniculata,* (Bentham) Troupin and spp. JULBERNARDIA, MUA (Tanzania)			T		
Lespedeza Michx. spp. LESPEDEZA		N		N	(S)
Lotus corniculatus L. BIRD'S-FOOT TREFOIL	N	N		NT(S)	(S)
Medicago L. spp.	N	N	NS	NTS	S
Medicago sativa L. LUCERNE, ALFALFA	N	N	NS	NTS	S
Melilotus Miller spp. SWEET CLOVER, MELILOT	N	N		NTS	S
Melilotus alba Medicus WHITE SWEET CLOVER, WHITE MELILOT	N	N		NTS	S
Onobrychis viciifolia Scop. SAINFOIN	N	N		NS	(S)
Ornithopus sativus Brot. SERADELLA	N	N	NS	(S)	
Phaseolus L. spp. BEAN (RUNNER, BLACK-EYED, LIMA, etc.)	N	N	TS	NTS	(S)
Piscidia piscipula L. HA'BIN (Maya), JAMAICA DOGWOOD				T	
Pongamia pinnata Pierre		T			
Prosopis (*glandulosa* Torr. and spp.) MESQUITE			S	NTS	S
Prosopis juliflora DC.		T	S	NTS	
Psoralea pinnata L. BLUE PINE WOOD, TAYLORINA			(S)	(S)	S
Robinia pseudoacacia L. (also other spp.) ROBINIA, ACACIA, BLACK LOCUST	N	N	NS	NS	S
Sophora japonica L. PAGODA TREE	N	N		NS	(S)
Tamarindus indica L. (only species) TAMARIND		T	T	T(S)	
Trifolium spp.	N	N	NT	NTS	S
Trifolium alexandrinium L. EGYPTIAN CLOVER, BARSEEM, BERSEEM		N	N	NS	
Trifolium hybridum L. ALSIKE CLOVER	N			NTS	
Trifolium incarnatum L. CRIMSON CLOVER	N			NTS	S
Trifolium pratense L. RED CLOVER	N	N	N	NTS	S
Trifolium repens L. WHITE CLOVER	N	N	N	NTS	S
Trifolium resupinatum L. PERSIAN CLOVER	N			N(S)	
Vicia L. spp. VETCHES	N	N	N	NTS	(S)
Vicia faba L. FIELD BEAN, BROAD BEAN	N	N	N	NTS	(S)
Vicia villosa Roth HAIRY VETCH	N	N	N	NS	

	Europe	Asia	Africa	America	Oceania
Liliaceae					
Allium L. spp. ONION, LEEK, GARLIC, etc.	N	N	NS	NTS	S
Aloe L. spp. ALOE			TS	(S)	
Asparagus officinalis L. ASPARAGUS	N	N	N	NT(S)	S
Lythraceae					
Lythrum salicaria L. PURPLE LOOSESTRIFE	N	N	N	N(S)	S
Magnoliaceae					
Liriodendron tulipifera L. TULIP TREE, TULIP POPLAR	N	N		N(S)	
Malvaceae					
Gossypium (*hirsutum* L. and spp.) COTTON	N	NT	NT	NT(S)	
Musaceae					
Musa L. spp. BANANA, PLANTAIN, etc.		T	T	T(S)	T
Myrtaceae					
Eucalyptus L'Herit. spp.	N	N	NTS	NTS	TS
Eucalyptus albens Miq. ex Bentham WHITE BOX			S	TS	S
Eucalyptus calophylla R. Br. ex Lindl. MARRI			S	S	S
Eucalyptus camaldulensis Dehnh. (RIVER) RED GUM			TS	TS	S
Eucalyptus citriodora Hook. LEMON-SCENTED GUM			NTS	TS	S
*Eucalyptus cladocalyx F. Muell. SUGAR GUM			S		S
Eucalyptus diversicolor F. Muell. KARRI			S	S	S
*Eucalyptus globulus Labill. TASMANIAN BLUE GUM				T	
*Eucalyptus gomphocephala DC.	N	N	NTS	N	TS
Eucalyptus grandis Hill ex Marden			NTS	S	S
Eucalyptus hemiphloia F. Muell. ex Bentham GREY BOX				S	S
Eucalyptus leucoxylon F. Muell. BLUE GUM and other names			S	(S)	S
Eucalyptus loxophleba Bentham YORK GUM					S
Eucalyptus maculata Hook. SPOTTED GUM			TS	(S)	S
Eucalyptus marginata Sm. JARRAH				S	S
Eucalyptus melliodora A. Cunn. ex Schau. YELLOW BOX			TS	S	S
Eucalyptus obliqua L'Herit. STRINGY BARK				S	S
Eucalyptus paniculata Sm. GREY IRONBARK			NTS	TS	S
Eucalyptus platypus Hook. MOORT					S
Eucalyptus robusta Sm. SWAMP MESSMATE			TS	TS	S
Eucalyptus rudis Endl. FLOODED GUM				(S)	S
Eucalyptus siderophloia Bentham BROAD-LEAVED IRONBARK				(S)	S
Eucalyptus sideroxylon A. Cunn. ex Bentham MUGGA, RED IRONBARK			TS	(S)	S

	Europe	Asia	Africa	America	Oceania
Eucalyptus tereticornis Sm.					
FOREST RED GUM			TS	TS	S
Eucalyptus viminalis Labill.					
MANNA GUM, WHITE GUM			TS	TS	S
Eucalyptus wandoo Blakely WANDOO					S
Leptospermum scoparium J. R. et G. Forst.					
and spp. MANUKA, TI TREE, TEA TREE					S
Melaleuca leucadendron L. CAJEPUT		T		T(S)	S
Metrosideros excelsa Soland. ex Gaertn.					
POHUTUKAWA					S
Metrosideros umbellata Cav. *robusta* A. Cunn.					
RATA					S
Myrtus communis L. MYRTLE	N	N		(S)	
Tristania conferta R. Br. (and spp.) SCRUB BOX				(S)	S
Syzygium Gaertn. spp.		T			
Nyssaceae					
Nyssa Gronov. ex. L. spp. TUPELO		T		N(S)	
Nyssa aquatica L.				N(S)	
Onagraceae					
Chamaenerion angustifolium (L.) Scop.					
ROSEBAY WILLOWHERB, FIREWEED	N	N		N	S
Palmaceae					
Cocos nucifera L. COCONUT PALM		T	T	T(S)	T
Roystonea (*regia* H.B.K. and spp.)					
ROYAL PALMS		T	T	T	(T)
Serenoa repens (Bartr.) Small, also other spp.					
SAW PALMETTO				N	
Pedaliaceae					
Sesamum orientale L. SESAME		T	T	T(S)	
Pinaceae					
Abies alba Miller SILVER FIR	N			(S)	
Abies bornmuellerana Mattfeld	N				
Larix decidua Miller LARCH	N			(S)	
Picea abies (L.) Karsten SPRUCE	N			(S)	
Pinus halepensis Miller	N			S	
Pinus mugo Turra MOUNTAIN PINE	N			S	
Pinus nigra Arnold AUSTRIAN PINE	N			S	
Pinus sylvestris L. SCOTS PINE	N			S	
Polygonaceae					
Antigonon leptopus Hook. and Arn.					
CORAL VINE				T(S)	
Erigonum fasciculatum Bentham WILD BUCKWHEAT				N	
Fagopyrum esculentum Moench BUCKWHEAT	N	N	S	NT(S)	

	Europe	Asia	Africa	America	Oceania
Gymnopodium antigonoides (Robinson) Blake DZIDZILCHE (Maya)				T	
Polygonum L. spp. BISTORT, HEARTSEASE, etc.	N	N	NT	NT(S)	S
Proteaceae					
Banksia L. spp. BANKSIA					S
Banksia menziesii, B. prionotes Menzies, ORANGE BANKSIA					S
Dryandra sessilis, also other spp. PARROT BUSH					S
Grevillea (*robusta* A. Cunn. and 230 spp.) GREVILLEA			T(S)	NTS	S
Knightea excelsa R. Br. REWAREWA, NEW ZEALAND HONEYSUCKLE					S
Protea L. spp. PROTEA			TS		
Rhamnaceae					
Rhamnus L. spp. BUCKTHORN	N	N		N(S)	
Rhamnus frangula Miller ALDER BUCKTHORN	N	N		N(S)	
Rosaceae					
Crataegus L. (*oxycantha* Thuill. and spp.) HAWTHORN	N	N		N(S)	S
Eriobotrya japonica Lindl. LOQUAT		T		T(S)	
Malus Mill./*Pyrus* L./*Prunus* L. spp. POME and STONE TREE FRUIT (APPLE, PEAR, PLUM, CHERRY)	N	N	(S)	NT(S)	S
Rubus fruticosus L. BLACKBERRY, BRAMBLE	N	N		N	S
Rubus idaeus L. RASPBERRY	N	N		NS	S
Rubiaceae					
Calycophyllum candidissimum (Vahl) DC. DAGAME (Spanish)				T(S)	
Coffea (*arabica* L. and spp.) COFFEE		TS	T	T(S)	
Rutaceae					
Citrus aurantium L. ORANGE	N	NT	NTS	NTS	S
Citrus L. other spp. LEMON, GRAPEFRUIT LIME, CITRON, etc.	N	N	NT	NTS	S
Salicaceae					
Salix L. (500 spp.) WILLOW	N	N	S	N(S)	S
Sapindaceae					
Euphoria longan (Lour.) Steud. LONGAN, LENGENG		T		T(S)	
Nephelium litchi Comb. – *Litchi chinensis* Sonn. LITCHI, LYCHEE		T	T	(S)	
Sapindus mukorossi Gaertn. possibly other spp. SOAPNUT		T		(T)	

166 *A Book of Honey*

	Europe	Asia	Africa	America	Oceania
Scrophulariaceae					
Scrophularia L. spp. FIGWORT	N	N		N	
Simarubaceae					
Ailanthus altissima SWINGLE, TREE OF HEAVEN		T		N(S)	
Sterculiaceae					
Dombeya rotundifolia (Hochst.) Planch. and					
spp. DOMBEYA		T	T	T	
Tamaricaceae					
Tamarix L. spp. TAMARISK	N	N	N	N(S)	
Tiliaceae					
Tilia L. spp. LIME, LINDEN, BASSWOOD	N	N		NS	S
Tilia americana L. BASSWOOD				N(S)	
Triumfetta rhomboidaea Jacq. and spp.					
TRIUMFETTA			T	T	T
Umbelliferae					
Anthriscus cerefolium (L.) Hoffm.					
COW PARSLEY	N	N	N	N(S)	
Daucus carota L. CARROT	N	N	N	N(S)	
Foeniculum vulgare Miller FENNEL	N			(S)	S
Heracleum sphondylium L. HOGWEED, COW					
PARSNIP	N	N	N	N(S)	
Verbenaceae					
Avicennia nitida Jacq. BLACK MANGROVE				T	(S)
Citharexylum Mill. spp. FIDDLEWOOD, etc.				T(S)	
Lippia Houst. ex L. spp. CARPET GRASS, etc.		N	T	NTS	
Vitex L. spp.		T	T	NT	(S)

Many of the plants in the above Table are named in Table 1.4/1 of the *Comprehensive survey*, which describes the plants briefly, and gives characteristics of their honeys and also, where possible, their honey-yielding potential. Plants marked * are new to the present list. For some of the less well documented areas, inclusion of additional information here has been made possible by the active collaboration of the following: Shri C. V. Thakar (Asia), Dr. M. T. Chandler and M. F. Johannsmeier (Africa T and S), Professor L. S. Gonçalves and Ing. Susana C. Peppino (America T and S), and G. M. Walton (Oceania T and S).

Table 2. Summary of age-linked stages in the life of a worker bee in summer

The ages entered for the adult bee are examples only. All are flexible in normal colony conditions, and highly flexible in abnormal conditions; an individual bee may show several different behaviour patterns on the same day.

Age (days) Stage	Food required	Other conditions	Behaviour
Brood Stage: DAY 0 = DAY EGG IS LAID			
0–3 egg	none	temp. *c* 34°C	none
3–8 larva	bee milk, then pollen + honey	temp. *c* 34°C	eats, moves in open cell
8–9 larva	none	temp. *c* 34°C	spins cocoon in sealed cell
9–21 prepupa, pupa	none	near 34°C	none

Adult Stage: DAY 0 = DAY OF EMERGENCE FROM CELL = DAY 21 OF BROOD STAGE

0–20 'house bee' i.e. remaining in the hive; preferring darkness to light; subdivided as follows:

0–5 'young bee'	pollen + honey		cleans cells
5–10 'nurse bee'	honey/nectar	hypopharyngeal glands secrete bee milk	feeds larvae
10–15 'building bee'	honey/nectar	wax glands developed	builds comb, caps cells
15–20 'guard bee'	honey/nectar	venom glands developed	guards hive (a few days only, or not at all)
20–30 'honey-making bee'	honey/nectar	hypopharyngeal glands secrete invertase	elaborates nectar etc. into honey
20–35+ to death 'field bee'	honey/nectar	flight muscles developed; attracted to light, not darkness	after short orientation flights, forages for pollen, nectar, etc., also (some bees) for water, or for propolis (and works with propolis in hive)

168 A Book of Honey

Table 3. Life span of worker bees in relation to brood rearing

Bees emerged on 20th of	Average life span in weeks (summer + winter + next spring)	Amount of brood reared compared with April
April	3½	100%
May	4	96%
June	4	83%
July	4½	56%
August	8 + 17 + 4 = 29	38%
September	5½ + 17 + 4½ = 27	21%
October	2 + 17 + 5 = 24	5%

The above results were obtained in 1972 in Tashkent, where winters are rather warm and summers hot. The drop in life expectancy from August to October could possibly be linked with decreasing pollen supplies through those months.

Table 4. Average amounts (%) of the major constituents of honey, as reported from studies in four countries. The final column gives the lowest and highest individual values for the 1063 honeys.

	Romania 1955	USSR 1963	USA 1962	Australia 1974	Range
Fructose	38·4	37·4	38·2	43·3	21·7 – 53·9
Glucose	34·0	35·9	31·3	30·2	20·4 – 44·4
Sucrose	3·1	2·1	1·3	2·5	0·0 – 7·6
F + G + S	75·5	75·4	70·8	76·0	
Water	16·5	18·6	17·2	15·6	13·4 – 26·6
F + G + S + W*	92·0	94·0	88·0	91·6	
No. samples	257	217	490	99	1063

* The most important of the minor constituents are indicated by the US averages:
reducing disaccharides calculated as maltose	7·3% (2·7–16·0)
higher sugars	1·5% (0·1–8·5)
total acid (as gluconic)	0·57% (0·17–1·17)
ash	0·17% (0·02–1·03)
nitrogen	0·94% (0·00–0·13)

Table 5. Complete list of sugars whose presence has so far been established or reliably inferred in honey.

---

monosaccharides (70% of honey):

glucose (dextrose)   fructose (laevulose)

disaccharides:

sucrose (1–3% of honey)

reducing disaccharides, calculated as maltose (7% of honey):

maltose	nigerose	gentiobiose
*iso*maltose	turanose	laminaribiose
maltulose	kojibiose	leucrose
*iso*maltulose	neotrehalose	

trisaccharides and higher sugars (1·5% of honey):

melezitose	erlose	1-kestose
raffinose	dextrantriose	panose
*iso*panose	maltotriose	*iso*maltotriose
*iso*maltotetraose	*iso*maltopentaose	3-α-*iso*maltosylglucose
6^G-α-glucosylsucrose	centose	
arabogalactomannan		

Table 6. Aroma constituents of honey

Alcohols	Ketones and aldehydes	Acids and their esters	
methanol	formaldehyde	formic	methyl ethyl
ethanol	acetaldehyde	acetic	methyl ethyl propyl *iso*propyl
propan-1-ol	propionaldehyde	propionic	ethyl
propan-2-ol	dimethyl ketone (acetone)	—	—
butan-1-ol	butyraldehyde	butyric	methyl ethyl *iso*amyl
*iso*butanol (2-methylpropan-1-ol)	*iso*butyraldehyde	—	—
butan-2-ol	methyl ethyl ketone (butan-2-one)	—	—
pentan-1-ol	valeraldehyde	valeric	methyl ethyl
pentan-2-ol	—	—	—
2-methylbutan-1-ol	—	—	—
*iso*pentanol (3-methylbutan-1-ol)	*iso*valeraldehyde	*iso*valeric	methyl
3-methylbutan-2-ol	—	—	—
—	caproaldehyde	—	—
—	—	gluconic	methyl
—	methacrolein	—	—
—	diacetyl	—	—
—	acetoin	—	—
benzyl alcohol	benzaldehyde	benzoic	methyl ethyl
2-phenylethanol	—	phenylacetic	methyl ethyl
3-phenylpropan-1-ol	—	—	—
4-phenylbutan-1-ol	—	—	—
furfuryl alcohol	furfural	—	—

The above information is taken from Table 5.82/1 of the *Comprehensive survey* and Table 14 of *Der Honig* (see *Further Reading*, Chapter 3).

Table 7. Upper limit on the Pfund scale for different colours of honey, according to Australian, Canadian and US standards. The final column gives the optical density* of honey corresponding to the Pfund readings that constitute colour-class boundaries in the USA.

Colour description	Australia	Canada	USA	Optical density
water white	—	—	8 mm	0·0945
extra white	17 mm	13 mm	17 mm	0·189
white	34 mm	30 mm	34 mm	0·378
extra light amber	50 mm	—	50 mm	0·595
golden	—	50 mm	—	—
light amber	65 mm	85 mm	85 mm	1·389
amber	90 mm	—	114 mm	3·008
dark amber	114 mm	114 mm	over 114 mm	—
dark	—	over 114 mm	—	—

* measured with light of wavelength 560 nm, using a layer of honey-glycerine solution 3·15 cm thick, with glycerine as a blank.

Table 8. Inactivation of enzymes in honey at different temperatures. Temperatures listed below reduce enzyme levels to half, in the period stated.

Temperature		Half-life	
°C	°F	Diastase	Invertase
10	50	34 years	26 years
20	68	4 years	2 years
30	86	200 days	83 days
40	104	31 days	10 days
50	122	5 days	1 day
60	140	1 day	5 hours
70	158	5 hours	47 minutes
80	176	1 hour	9 minutes

Table 9. Minerals in US honeys, in order of importance, as identified in an extensive study by Schuette and his colleagues. On the right are trace elements found by various research workers.

Mineral element	Average in light honey (ppm)	Average in dark honey (ppm)	Trace elements identified in honey
potassium	205	1676	chromium
			lithium
chlorine	52	113	nickel
			lead
sulphur	58	100	tin
			zinc
sodium	18	76	osmium
			beryllium
calcium	49	51	vanadium
			zirconium
phosphorus	35	47	silver
			barium
magnesium	19	35	gallium
			bismuth
silicon (as SiO_2)	9	14	gold
			germanium
iron	2·4	9·4	strontium
manganese	0·3	4·1	
copper	0·3	0·6	

Table 10. Average glucose/water ratio for honeys grouped according to their granulation after 6 months of undisturbed storage at 23–28°C, in ½-lb or 1-lb jars (0·23 or 0·46 kg). The honeys had been pre-treated 'to clarity, as indicated by the polariscope', i.e. all crystals had been dissolved.

Glucose/water ratio	Granulation after 6 months	No. samples
1·58	none	96
1·76	few scattered crystals	114
1·79	1·5–3 mm layer of crystals	67
1·83	6–12 mm layer of crystals	68
1·86	few clumps of crystals	19
1·99	¼ of depth granulated	32
1·98	½ of depth granulated	19
2·06	¾ of depth granulated	16
2·16	complete soft granulation	18
2·24	complete hard granulation	28

Table 11. Relative density (specific gravity) and calculated values for the refractive index of honey at water contents from 13% to 21%. Figures are taken from a fuller table in the *Comprehensive survey*.

Water content (%)	Relative density		Refractive index	
	(20°C)	(60°F)	(20/20°C)	(60/60°F)
13·0	1·4457	1·4472	1·5044	1·5053
14·0	1·4404	1·4419	1·5018	1·5027
15·0	1·4350	1·4365	1·4992	1·5002
16·0	1·4295	1·4310	1·4966	1·4976
17·0	1·4237	1·4252	1·4940	1·4951
18·0	1·4171	1·4187	1·4915	1·4925
19·0	1·4101	1·4117	1·4890	1·4900
20·0	1·4027	1·4043	1·4865	1·4875
21·0	1·3950	1·3966	1·4840	1·4850

Table 12. Coefficient of viscosity of honey and 'ease of flow'.
A. Variation with water content at constant temperature (25°C, 77°F), honey from white clover, *Trifolium repens*.

Water content	Coeff. of viscosity (poise)	'Ease of flow'*	Water content	Coeff. of viscosity (poise)	'Ease of flow'*
13·7%	420	0·11	18·2%	48	1·0
14·2%	269	0·18	19·1%	35	1·4
15·5%	138	0·35	20·2%	20	2·4
17·1%	69	0·70	21·5%	14	3·5

B. Variation with temperature at constant water content (16·1%), honey from sweet clover, *Melilotus*.

Temperature		Coeff. of viscosity (poise)	'Ease of flow'*
°C	°F		
13·7	56·7	600·0	0·3
20·6	69·1	189·6	1·0
29·0	84·2	68·4	3
39·4	102·9	21·4	9
48·1	118·6	10·7	18
71·1	159·8	2·6	73

* Entries under 'Ease of flow' here are, arbitrarily, the reciprocal of the coefficient of viscosity, taking the coefficient as unity at 18·2% water content and at 25°C.

Table 13. Nutrients in honey in relation to human requirements. This table is taken from Table 8.4/1 of the *Comprehensive survey*, entries in Column 3 being derived from other data in that book. Figures in Columns 4 and 5 relate to an adult man; those for an adult woman, or for a person under 20, are in general the same or lower.

1 *Nutrient*	*2* *Unit*	*3* *Average amount in 100 g honey*	*4* *Recommended daily intake UK**	*5* *Recommended daily intake USA*
Energy equivalent	kcal	304	2,600–3,600	2,800
Vitamins:				
A	i.u.		2,500	5,000
B₁ (Thiamine)	mg	0·004–0·006	1·1–1·4	1·5
B₂ complex:				
Riboflavin	mg	0·02–0·06	1·7	1·7
Nicotinic acid (niacin)	mg equiv.	0·11–0·36	18	20
B₆ (Pyridoxine)	mg	0·008–0·32	(1–2)	2·0
Pantothenic acid	mg	0·02–0·11	(10–20)	10
Folic acid	mg		0·05–0·1	0·4
B₁₂	μg		3–4	6
C (Ascorbic acid)	mg	2·2–2·4	30	60
D	i.u.		100	400
E	i.u.		(10 mg)	30
H (Biotin)	mg			0·3
Minerals:				
Calcium	g	0·004–0·03	0·5	1·0
Chlorine	g	0·002–0·02	(5–9)	
Copper	mg	0·01–0·1	(2·0–2·5)	2·0
Iodine	mg		0·15	0·15
Iron	mg	0·1–3·4	10	18
Magnesium	mg	0·7–13	(150–450)	400
Manganese	mg	0·02–10	(5–10)	
Phosphorus	g	0·002–0·06	(1·2–2·0)	1·0
Potassium	g	0·01–0·47	(2–4)	
Sodium	g	0·0006–0·04	(3–6)	
Zinc	mg	0·2–0·5	(10–15)	15

* Figures in brackets indicate actual daily intakes, *not* recommended daily intakes.

Table 14. Approximate average figures relating to annual world honey production and consumption, by continent.

Figures are for 1970 or earlier: they are taken from the *Comprehensive survey*, which gives further details and entries for individual countries. Overall production has since risen by about 25%, but no current detailed figures are available.

	OLD WORLD				NEW WORLD			TOTAL
1. Continent	Europe*	USSR	Asia*	Africa	N America	S/C America	Oceania	
2. Area in 1000 km²	4,682	22,400	27,896	32,315	19,636	20,785	7,956	135,670
3. No. beekeepers in 1000s	1,367	1,150	900	2,526	435	235	12	6,625
4. No. colonies of bees in 1000s	12,983	10,000	6,000	12,000	4,754	4,000	684	50,421
5. Honey production in tons	120,680	103,000	73,000	82,700	125,200	102,000	23,850	630,430
6. Honey yield per colony in kg	9	11	12	6	26	25	35	12·5
7. No. colonies per beekeeper	9·5	8	7	6	14	17	56	8
8. Honey production per beekeeper in kg	90	90	70	30	300	50	2,000	95
9. Colony density per km²	2·8	0·4	0·2	0·4	0·24	0·19	0·09	0·4
10. Honey consumption per capita in kg	0·4	0·5	0·004	0·26	0·7	0·1	0·5	0·17
11. Sugar consumption per capita in kg	36	45	7	11	49	42	57	20

* excluding USSR

Further reading

Books that provide useful further reading on the subject of each chapter are listed below. Those out of print in 1980 are included where no book in print can substitute for them. Similarly, books in languages other than English are included where they alone provide what is likely to be wanted.

In order to help readers to gain access to books recommended, they are marked, where appropriate, 'from IBRA' (sold by the Association in 1980) or 'out of print' (out of print in 1980). Books not marked should be available through booksellers, and many of the books are likely to be stocked by public libraries.

Further information on most subjects dealt with briefly here can be found in *Honey: a comprehensive survey*, edited by Eva Crane. This book, with 608 pages, was published in 1975 in London by William Heinemann Ltd in co-operation with the International Bee Research Association (IBRA); it was sold out within a year, and in 1976 was reprinted with corrections. It is referred to in the present book as the *Comprehensive survey*. A German book by Anna Maurizio and others, published in 1975, is referred to by its title *Der Honig*.

The *Comprehensive survey* will usually provide a reference to the original publications on which a statement in the present book is based, and it lists details of 1,400 such references, together with the serial number of an English summary in the journal *Apicultural Abstracts*, published since 1950 by the International Bee Research Association. Where the present book refers to more recent scientific work, the author is named and the year of the original publication is given (usually 1975 or later), to enable those interested to trace the publication through *Apicultural Abstracts*.

Chapter 1. Bees: the honey producers

1. Butler, C. G. (1974), *The world of the honeybee*. London: Collins, rev. edn., 226 pp., from IBRA.
2. Frisch, K. von (1966), *The dancing bees*. London: Methuen, 2nd edn., 198 pp., out of print.
3. Frisch, K. von (1967), *The dance language and orientation of bees*. Cambridge, Mass.: Harvard University Press, 566 pp., from IBRA.
4. Dadant & Sons (1975), *The hive and the honey bee*. Hamilton, Ill.: Dadant & Sons, 740 pp, from IBRA.
5. Free, J. B. (1977), *The social organization of honeybees*. London: Edward Arnold, 68 pp., from IBRA.

6. Procter, M.; Yeo, P. (1973), *The pollination of flowers*. London: Collins, 418 pp., from IBRA.

7. Meeuse, B. J. D. (1961), *The story of pollination*. New York: Ronald Press, 243 pp.

8. Powell, J. (1979), *The world of a beehive*. London: Faber & Faber, 144 pp., from IBRA.

9. *Honey: a comprehensive survey,* from IBRA, see Chapter 2: How bees make honey *by* Anna Maurizio.

Book 1, first written in 1954, is a readable introduction to honeybees in general; 2 (simple) and 3 (more advanced) are clearly written books on a wider subject than their titles suggest. Book 4 is the latest revision of a multi-author book that is excellent value; it is the successor to the book first published by L.L. Langstroth in 1853. Chapters 2–7 are on bees, and many other chapters also relate to subjects covered in the present book. Of books 6 and 7, 6 is the fuller and more useful, but 7 is a popular and vivid introduction. Book 8 is the most recent available; Book 9 is described above.

Chapter 2. Plants: the honey resources

1. Howes, F. N. (1945, reprinted 1979), *Plants and beekeeping*. London: Faber & Faber, 236 pp., from IBRA.

2. Pellett, F. C. (1945, reprinted 1977), *American honey plants*. Hamilton, Ill.: Dadant & Sons, 467 pp., from IBRA.

3. Maurizio, Anna; Grafl, Ina (1980), *Trachtpflanzenbuch* [Book of bee plants]. Munich: Ehrenwirth Verlag, 2nd edn., 288 pp., from IBRA.

4. Kloft, W.; Maurizio, Anna; Kaeser, W. (1965), *Das Waldhonigbuch* [The honeydew book]. Munich: Ehrenwirth Verlag, 2nd edn., 218 pp., out of print.

5. Percival, Mary S. (1965), *Floral biology*. Oxford: Pergamon Press, 243 pp.

6. *Honey: a comprehensive survey*, from IBRA, see Chapter 1: The flowers honey comes from *by* Eva Crane.

Book 1 relates to Britain and 2 to the USA; 3 is the best book for the bee plants of Europe in general, and 4 the best book on honeydew honey. Book 5 explains the intimate relationships between flowers and insects.

Chapter 3. Constituents and characteristics of honey

1. *Honey: a comprehensive survey*, from IBRA, see Chapters 5 and 6: Composition of honey, Physical characteristics of honey *by* J. W. White, Jr.; Chapter 7: Microscopy of honey *by* Anna Maurizio

2. Maurizio, Anna and others (1975), *Der Honig* [Honey]. Stuttgart: Eugen Ulmer Verlag, 212 pp., from IBRA.

3. International Commission for Bee Botany of the IUBS (1978) *Methods of melissopalynology*, rev. edn., IBRA Reprint M95, 19 pp., from IBRA.

4. Deans, A. S. C. (1957), *Survey of British honey sources*. London: Bee Research Association, 20 pp., out of print.

5. Munro, S. (1977), *Honey*. London: Franklin Watts, 48 pp, from IBRA.

On honey itself, the *Comprehensive survey* provides the fullest and most up-to-date account in English. The German book (2) covers some of the same ground, with a fully documented and competently written text. Item 3 provides instructions for pollen analysis of honey, and 4 gives results of pollen analysis of 854 honeys from Britain and Ireland. The final book, well illustrated, is written for children.

Chapter 4. Honey in the home

1. Elkon, Juliette (1955), *The honey cookbook*. New York: Alfred A. Knopf, 162 pp.

2. Berto, Hazel (1972), *Cooking with honey*. New York: Crown Publishers, 234 pp.

3. Lo Pinto, Maria (1972), *Eat honey and live longer*. New York: Twayne Publishers, 174 pp., out of print.

4. Wilhelm, Maxine (1965), *Honey cook book*. Erick, Okla.: Wilhelm Honey Farm, 126 pp.

5. Australian Honey Board (1973), *The Australian honey recipe book*. Sydney: Australian Honey Board, 40 pp.

6. Paillon, P. (1960), *La fabrication des produits alimentaires*. Paris: Girardot, 238 pp., out of print.

7. Acton, B.; Duncan, P. (1965), *Making mead*. Andover, Hants.: Amateur Winemaker, 60 pp.

8. Tannahill, Reay (1973), *Food in history*. London: Eyre Methuen, 384 pp., out of print; Paladin Books (paperback) 1975.

9. Wilson, C. Anne (1973), *Food and drink in Britain from the Stone Age to recent times*. London: Constable, 426 pp.

10. *Honey: a comprehensive survey*, from IBRA, see Chapter 15: Uses and products of honey *by* R. B. Willson and Eva Crane; Chapter 16: Wines from the fermentation of honey *by* R. A. Morse and K. H. Steinkraus.

Book 1 is the best honey cookery book; 2 includes text matter about the use of honey, as well as recipes; so does 3, which covers food, cosmetics and remedies. No. 4 is a homely loose-leaf collection of recipes. All are for American palates and in American measures. Book 6 gives much information not available elsewhere. Books 8 and 9 are both available in paperback and are scholarly works of wide interest.

Chapter 5. Honey in the past and present

1. Fraser, H. M. (1951), *Beekeeping in antiquity*. London: University of London Press, 2nd edn., 145 pp., out of print.

2. Fraser, H. M. (1958), *History of beekeeping in Britain*. London: Bee Research Association, 106 pp., out of print.

3. Galton, Dorothy (1971), *Survey of a thousand years of beekeeping in Russia*. London: Bee Research Association, 90 pp., from IBRA.

4. Pager, H. (1973), *Rock paintings in Southern Africa showing bees and honey hunting*. IBRA Reprint M68, 8 pp., from IBRA.

5. Pager, H. (1976), *Cave paintings suggest honey hunting activities in Ice Age times*. IBRA Reprint M85, 8 pp., from IBRA.

6. Dams, Lya R. (1978), *Bees and honey-hunting scenes in the Mesolithic rock art of Eastern Spain*. IBRA Reprint M93, 9 pp., from IBRA.

7. Crane, Eva (1979), *Directory of the world's beekeeping museums*. IBRA Reprint M87, 15 pp., from IBRA.

8. *Honey: a comprehensive survey*, from IBRA, see Chapter 19: History of honey *by* Eva Crane; Chapter 18: The language of honey *by* D. E. Le Sage; Chapter 4: The world's honey production *by* Eva Crane.

Books 1 and 2 are small classics of their kind. Book 3 opens up a little-known world both past and present, and Reprints 4–6 an earlier and more primitive one. Posters are available from the IBRA of the rock paintings in figs. 17 and 18.

Item 7 provides a mini-guidebook to museums in 22 countries where historical bee and honey materials can be seen.

Chapter 6. Bees and honey in the minds of men

1. Ransome, Hilda M. (1937), *The sacred bee in ancient times and folklore*. London: George Allen & Unwin, 308 pp., out of print.

2. Beck, B. F. (1938), *Honey and health*. New York: Robert M. McBride, 272 pp., out of print.

3. Hodgson, Natalie B. (1973), *Children's books on bees and beekeeping*. IBRA Bibliography No. 14, 55 pp., from IBRA.

4. Bessler, J. G. (1886), *Geschichte der Bienenzucht* [History of beekeeping]. Stuttgart, Germany: W. Kohlhammer, 275 pp., out of print.

5. International Bee Research Association (1979), *British bee books: a bibliography 1500–1976*. London: IBRA, 270 pp., from IBRA.

Books 1 and 2 are valuable sources of information on folklore and legend, superstition and custom; book 2 was in preparation at the same time as 1, but without knowledge of it. Bibliography 3 contains an annotated chronological list of 353 books, which are set in perspective by the same author's *Guide to children's literature on bees and beekeeping*, IBRA Reprint M70, 18 pp. (1973). Book 4 includes sections on bee mythology and history, and also one on German bee poetry. I do not know any book on bees and honey in English literature; *A bee melody* by H. Brown (1923) is perhaps the nearest. The thesis by Dr. A. E. Fife, referred to in the text, is not available for sale, but a photocopy is in the IBRA Library. Book 5 is a recently published key to books on all six chapters.

Appendix 1. Producing your own honey

1. Ministry of Agriculture (England & Wales) Bulletin No. 9 (1976) *Beekeeping*, 26 pp.; Bulletin No. 206 (1975) *Swarming of bees*. 38 pp.; both from IBRA.

2. Sammataro, D.; Avitabile, A. (1978) *The beekeeper's handbook*. Dexter, Michigan, USA: Peach Mountain Press, 131 pp., from IBRA.

3. Vernon, F. (1976), *Beekeeping*. London: Hodder & Stoughton (Teach Yourself Books), 212 pp., from IBRA.

4. Jaycox, E. R. (1976), *Beekeeping in the midwest*. London: University of Illinois Press, 160 pp., from IBRA.

5. *The hive and the honeybee* (item 4 under Chapter 1 above) has Chapter 11: For the beginner *by* W. A. Stephen.

6. Bielby, W. B. (1977), *Home honey production*. Wakefield: EP Publishing, 72 pp., from IBRA.

7. Frankland, A. W. (1976), *Bee sting allergy*. IBRA Reprint M88, 6 pp., from IBRA.

8. Bee Research Association (1968), *Clearing bees from honey supers*. IBRA Reprint T1, 12 pp., from IBRA.

9. Johansson, T. S. K.; Johansson, M.P. (1978), *Some important operations in bee management*. London: International Bee Research Association, 145 pp., from IBRA.

10. *Honey: a comprehensive survey*, from IBRA, see Chapter 9: Processing and storing liquid honey *by* G. F. Townsend; Chapter 10: Producing finely granulated or creamed honey *by* E. J. Dyce; Chapter 11: Producing various forms of comb honey *by* C. E. Killion.

The bulletins in 1 provide good instruction at modest prices; so does book 3, which incorporates recent research findings that provide a basis for beekeeping practice; book 4 is similar, relating to the USA. Item 5 covers bare essentials. Book 6 includes modern beekeeping using hives without frames, at low cost. Reprint 7 is a specialist's account of this rare but important condition. Reprint 8 explains the various well tried methods for harvesting honey, and book 10 is a mine of well documented information with full references to the researches on which it is based. Book 2 is an explicit, well illustrated paperback for the beginner.

Index

NOTE. Entries with very general initial words – bee(s), hive(s), honey, honeybees – are used as little as possible; information on, e.g., liquid honey will be found under the word liquid.

The Index does not include plants mentioned only in fig. 9 or Table 1, or chemical substances mentioned only in Tables 5–13 of Appendix 2. With the above exceptions, page numbers are entered under the common name of a plant, which also leads to the botanical name either in the Index (e.g. almond) or on the first page cited (e.g. acacia). The botanical name of each plant is indexed, e.g. *Allium cepa* = onion. Any page referring to honey from a specific plant is included under the common name of the plant.

Page numbers in bold type indicate an extensive list. Authors (but not titles) of books listed in *Further reading* are indexed.

There are the following text-references to the Tables:

Table	Page	Table	Page	Table	Page
1	37–8	6	44	11	55
2	4–6	7	46–7	12	57
3	5–6	8	47–9	13	51, 95
4	39	9	51	14	124–7
5	41	10	53–4		

blackberry (*Rubus fruticosus*), 28, 30, 37, 73, 165
blackcurrant (*Ribes nigrum*), 22
blending honey, 46–7
blessing of bees/honey, 137, 150
Borago officinalis = borage, 30, 33, 34, 45, 61, 159
Boswell, James, 119
bracken (*Pteridium aquilinum*), 31, 32
bracket, 94
Brassica napus/rapa = rape
Brassica spp., 28, 160
Brazil, 26, 27, 114, 126
bread, 76–7
Britain/British Isles, 62, 63, 69–71, 111, 113, 129, 146, 152; *see also* England; Scotland; United Kingdom; Wales
brood, 1, 2, 3, 22, 108, 119, 167
  chamber, 122, 123
  nest, 1, 4, 6, 15, 119
  rearing, 5, 6, 7, 17, 168
Brooke, Rupert, 66
Brown, H., 179
buckwheat, 50, 59, 164
bumble bees, 19
Bumby, Mary Anna, 120
burns, 97
Bushman paintings, 105, 136
Butler, C. G., 176
Butler, Charles, 130

cakes, 72, 74–6, 80–5
calcium oxalate, 51
Calluna vulgaris = ling heather
calorific value of honey, 58–9
campanilla, 45, 160
Canada, 70, 124, 125, 171; *see also* American continent
candles, 114, 116, 138–9, 144, 160
cane hives, 113
cane sugar, 95, 117–18; *see also* sugar cane (plant)
capping cells, 18, 55, 167
Capsicum annuum = sweet pepper
carbohydrates *see* sugars
carpel, 31
Carthage, 141
Carvia callosa = karvi
Castanea sativa = Spanish/sweet chestnut
catalase, 47, 49

catkins, 4, 21
cells, capping, 18, 167
  honey in, 16–17, 55
Celtic languages, 93, 129
Centaurea cyanus = cornflower
Centaurea nigra = knapweed
centrifuging honey *see* extracting honey
Cerinthe minor = wax flower = honeywort, lesser
Chamaenerion angustifolium = rosebay willowherb
chamber, brood/honey, 121, 122, 123
charlock, 30, 160
'chastity' of bees, 138–9
Chaucer, Geoffrey, 142–3
cheese-honey icing, 72
cherry laurel (*Prunus laurocerasus*), 31
  sour, 28, 165
  sweet (*Prunus avium*), 22, 165
chestnut buds, 23
chestnut, horse, 28, 161
  Spanish/sweet, 30, 33, 43, 51, 61, 161
child nutrition, 95, 98, 132, 135, 137
children, books for, 179
chimpanzees, 105
China, 113, 117, 124, 125, 126, 135
chocolate, bees foraging on, 36
Christianity, 130, 135, 136–40, 144, 147; *see also* Bible, honey in; monastic communities
Church, Christian, bees as model for, 138–40, 144
Churchill, Sir Winston, 152–3
Cirsium spp. = thistle
citric acid, 35, 49
Citrullus vulgaris = watermelon
citrus (*Citrus* spp.) 33, 37, 48, 60, 73, 165 *see also* orange
clare, 94
clay hives, 111, 112, 113
clear honey *see* liquid honey
clover (*Trifolium* spp.), 17, 22, 28, 99, 153, 162
  red, 30, 33, 37, 45, 162
  white (*Trifolium repens*), 5, 30, 31, 37, 50, 62, 120, 162, 173; *see also* sweet clover (*Melilotus*)
cluster, winter, 6
Coca-Cola, bees using, 36
coconut (*Cocos nucifera*), 113, 164
cocoon, 167
coffee (*Coffea arabica*), 22, 165

184   *Index*